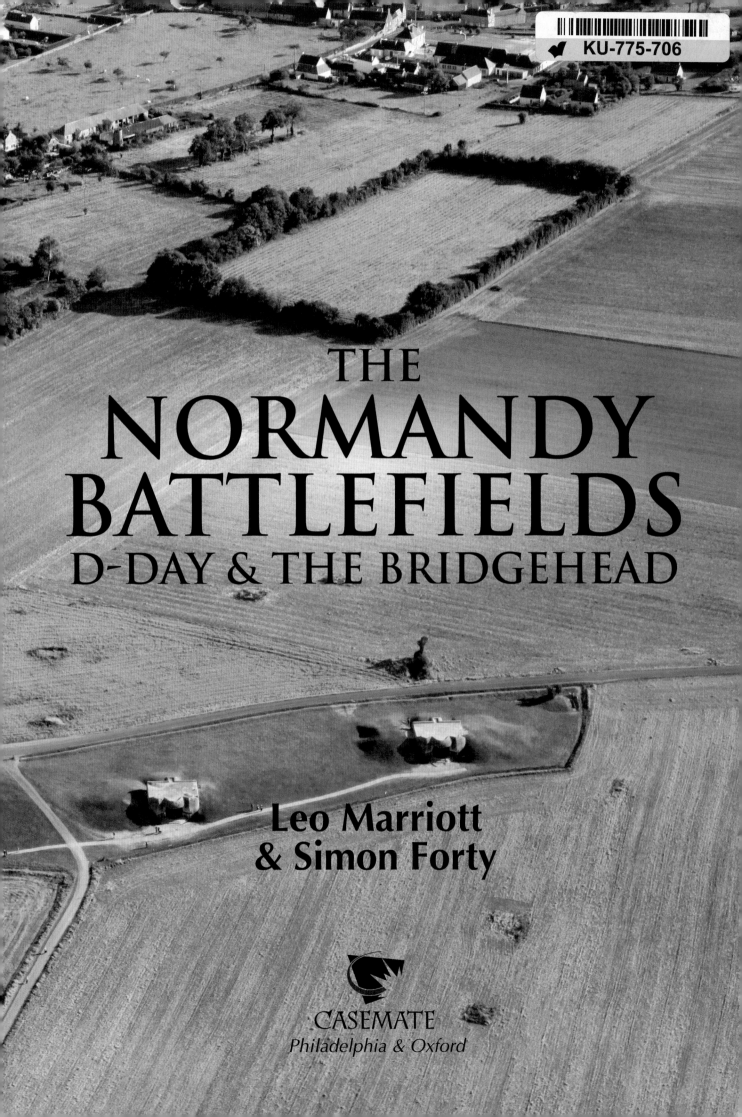

THE
NORMANDY
BATTLEFIELDS
D-DAY & THE BRIDGEHEAD

**Leo Marriott
& Simon Forty**

CASEMATE
Philadelphia & Oxford

Abbreviations and Glossary

AA(A) Anti-aircraft (artillery)
AEAF Allied Expeditionary Air Force
AB Airborne
ACM Air Chief Marshal
ADGB Air Defence Great Britain
Adm Admiral
AM Air Marshal
Armd Armored
A/Tk Anti-tank
Ausf *Ausfach* (model/type)
BARV Beach armored recovery vehicle
Bde Brigade
BLT Battalion landing team
Bn Battalion
C–i–C Commander-in-chief
CFPU Canadian Forces Photo Unit
COSSAC Chief of Staff to Supreme Allied Commander
Coy Company
DD Duplex Drive
Div Division
DZ Dropping zone (for paratroops)
Eureka beacon A ground-based transponder that was picked up by the Rebecca airborne transceiver and used to mark landing areas for airborne forces.
ESB Engineer Special Bde
FDT Fighter direction tenders
GIR Glider Infantry Regt
Ind Independent
Inf Infantry
K/MIA Killed/missing in action
LCA Landing craft, assault
LCG (L) Landing craft, gun (large)
LCI Landing craft, infantry
LCI (L) LCI (Large)
LCI(S) LCI (Small)
LCM Landing craft, mechanized—many different designs all based loosely on the 1920s British motor landing craft.
LCT Landing craft, tank
LCT (A) Landing craft, tank (armored)—used by the first wave they had extra armor protection and the two front tanks could fire ahead.
LCT (HE) Landing craft, tank, carrying M7 105mm SP guns (British)
LCT (R) Landing craft, tank (rocket)—armed with 3-inch RP-3 rockets
LCT (SP) Landing craft, tank, carrying 155mm SP guns (American)
LCVP Landing craft, vehicle, personnel—the Higgins boat
LSI/T Landing ship, infantry or tank—much larger than LCIs, these could carry around 20 tanks or 1,000 men (the largest nearly 2,000) plus landing craft
Lt-Col Lieutenant-colonel
Lt-Gen Lieutenant-general
LZ Landing zone (for gliders)
Maj-Gen Major-general
MG Machine gun
NSFCP Naval shore fire control party
Ord Ordnance
PIAT Projectile, Infantry, Anti-Tank
PIR Parachute Infantry Regt
Pl Platoon
PLUTO, Operation Pipelines under the ocean—the supply of petrol to Allied troops in Normandy. The first pipeline was a short one from tankers through Port en Bessin. Later, longer pipelines ran from the Isle of Wight to Cherbourg and between Dungeness and Ambleteuse near Boulogne
PoW prisoner of war
PzKpfw *Panzerkampfwagen* (tank)
Pz Div Panzer division
PzGr Panzer grenadier (motorized infantry)
QM Quartermaster
QORC Queen's Own Rifles of Canada
RAC Royal Armoured Corps
RAMC Royal Army Medical Corps
RASC Royal Army Service Corps
RCAF Royal Canadian Air Force
RCT Regimental combat team
RDG Royal Dragoon Guards
RE Royal Engineers
REME Royal Electrical and Mechanical Engineers
RCA Royal Canadian Artillery
RN Royal Navy
SHAEF Supreme Headquarters Allied Expeditionary Force
Sp *Sturzpunkt* (strongpoint)
SP self-propeled
SpS Special Service as in No 1 SpS Bde
Sqn Squadron
Tobruk or *Ringstellung* A concrete-reinforced foxhole, often a Bauform 201 or 58c, used as an observation post or MG position; often a part of a larger WN.
USAAF US Army Air Force
USN US Navy
WN *Widerstandnest* (pl *-er*) lit resistance nest: defensive position that combined bunkers, minefields, barbed wire, artillery, and machine guns

Published in the United States of America and Great Britain in 2014 by
CASEMATE PUBLISHERS
908 Darby Road, Havertown, PA 19083
and
10 Hythe Bridge Street, Oxford, OX1 2EW

ISBN 978-1-61200-231-6

Cataloging-in-publication data is available from the Library of Congress and the British Library.

10 9 8 7 6 5 4 3 2 1

Printed and bound in China

For a complete list of Casemate titles please contact:

CASEMATE PUBLISHERS (US)
Telephone (610) 853-9131, Fax (610) 853-9146
E-mail: casemate@casematepublishing.com

CASEMATE PUBLISHERS (UK)
Telephone (01865) 241249, Fax (01865) 794449
E-mail: casemate-uk@casematepublishing.co.uk

Previous page: *The battery at Longues between the landing beaches Omaha and Gold.*

Below: *Organized chaos! Gold Beach on D-Day.*

Note *Our left-hand page markers take the form of the totemic* Voie de la Liberté *(Liberty Road) 1944 markers. Opened in 1947, the idea of Guy de la Vasselais, it follows the route of Patton's Third Army, with markers from Utah Beach to Metz and on to Bastogne.*

CONTENTS

INTRODUCTION

"You are about to embark upon the Great Crusade, toward which we have striven these many months...In company with our brave Allies and brothers-in-arms on other Fronts, you will bring about the destruction of the German war machine, the elimination of Nazi tyranny over the oppressed peoples of Europe, and security for ourselves in a free world."

Dwight D. Eisenhower, address to Allied soldiers on June 6, 1944

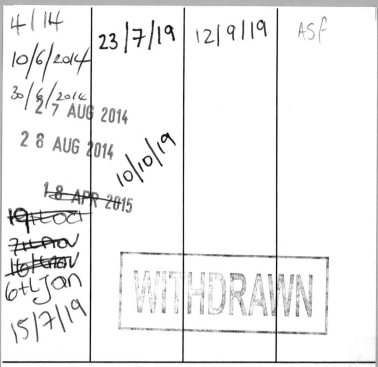

THE
NORMANDY
BATTLEFIELDS
D-DAY & THE BRIDGEHEAD

The extreme bravery of the troops who attacked on Omaha Beach is today marked by a monument commissioned by the French government to celebrate the 60th anniversary of the landings in 2004. Sculpted by Anilore Banon, the monument is in the surf at the join of Dog Red and Easy Green beaches at St. Laurent. The most heavily contested of the D-Day beaches, total US casualties on Omaha totalled around 2,000.

On May 10, 1940, an unstoppable torrent of German tanks and infantry burst through the supposedly impenetrable Ardennes forest on the Franco-Belgian border, and crossed the Meuse at Sedan. Supported by an aerial armada of fighters and dive-bombers, the German Panzer divisions raced westward, and in less than three weeks had the British Expeditionary Force and large elements of the French Army penned against the Channel coast. Over a period of several days up to June 4, 1940, British, French, Dutch, and Belgian vessels managed to evacuate over 338,000 British and French troops in what was termed the "miracle" of Dunkirk. However, even Winston Churchill himself warned the British people that they should not consider these momentous events to be victory.

It would be four long and arduous years, almost to the day, before the tide was irrevocably turned and Allied troops landed back in France with the strength and power to ensure the ultimate victory. On D–Day, June 6, 1944, over 150,000 British, Canadian, and American troops, supported by soldiers of many other nations, were landed over the Normandy beaches in Operation Overlord—the largest and most complex amphibious landing against organized opposition ever attempted. Such an operation was not put together overnight: its successful outcome was the result of years of meticulous planning, not to mention the arguments and differences in strategy which initially beset the Allied camp.

In the 12 months after Dunkirk Britain stood alone, secure in its island base thanks to the RAF victory in the Battle of Britain, but totally lacking the resources to mount a cross-Channel operation to take the fight back to continental Europe. In May 1941 Hitler turned his attention to the east when he launched Operation Barbarossa to invade the Soviet Union. While this brought Russia into the Allied camp, it was initially of little comfort as the Red Army was thrown back to the gates of Moscow and Britain was forced to divert vital supplies to its hard-pressed new ally.

December 7, 1941, proved to be a decisive turning point in the war as the Japanese Navy launched a surprise attack on Pearl Harbor and virtually eliminated the US Navy's battlefleet, declaring war shortly after. Subsequently, Japanese forces ran amok in the Western Pacific and South-East Asia with British and American forces suffering major and embarrassing defeats

before the situation could be stabilized. Significantly, Hitler declared war on the United States on December 11.

From the start, Churchill realized that the addition of American manpower and industrial might to the Allied cause meant that ultimate victory was assured. Prior to Pearl Harbor the United States, although nominally neutral, had provided Britain with assistance in the form of Lend-Lease supplies and active escorting of Atlantic convoys. In August 1941 Churchill and President Roosevelt, together with their military advisors, had already met at Placentia Bay, Newfoundland, to discuss possible Anglo-American co-operation. In the aftermath of Pearl Harbor, the position had changed and a further summit meeting, the Arcadia Conference, was held in Washington commencing on December 22, 1941, in which basic Allied strategies were discussed and agreed.

The most important outcome was the policy of "Germany First"—Allied efforts would prioritize on the defeat of Germany before that of Japan. Already the Russian leader, Josef Stalin, was calling for a second front to relieve pressure on his own forces, and the American generals were eager to do this, calling for a cross-Channel invasion of mainland Europe as early as 1942. Even at this point the Combined Chiefs of Staff considered the Marshall Memorandum, which called for a landing over the Normandy beaches in 1942, codenamed Operation Sledgehammer, to establish a beachhead which would then be reinforced in preparation for a major offensive and push towards the Rhine (Operation Roundup) in 1943. However, it soon became obvious that the necessary resources for such an operation would not be available on that timescale. With great reluctance the Americans eventually agreed to Operation Torch, the invasion of North Africa. In the event this

10

dovetailed nicely with the British Eighth Army's defeat of Rommel at the Battle of El Alamein in November 1942, and Axis forces were eventually driven out of Africa by May 1943. At least Torch had given the Allies valuable experience of planning and executing a major amphibious landing and had also given the US Army some hard-learned lessons on the realities of fighting against experienced German troops.

Even while fighting in North Africa was still in progress, a further Allied summit conference was held at Casablanca in January 1943. The most significant outcome of this was the adoption a policy whereby the war would only be brought to a conclusion by the unconditional surrender of all Axis nations and their forces. However, beneath the facade of Allied unity there were serious differences about the future strategic direction of the war. Concerned that Britain still lacked the resources to launch a major cross-Channel operation, Churchill persisted with the view that the allies should build on their success in North Africa to attack what he termed "the soft underbelly of Europe." The Americans were still eager to mount an operation against northern Europe in 1943: in fact, at one stage the US Navy C-in-C Admiral King proposed that all amphibious assets be transferred to the Pacific if an invasion of France was not going to take place in 1943. In the end Churchill's view prevailed but with some compromises. Some diversion of resources to Pacific operations was agreed but the Mediterranean strategy would continue with an Anglo-American invasion of Sicily in July 1943 (Operation Husky). The Americans hoped that this would be the last major operation in this theater but, as they feared, it led on to further landings in Italy and a long

campaign against German forces which lasted right to the end of European hostilities in May 1945, despite the Italian surrender in September 1943.

It was agreed at Casablanca to set up a Combined Planning Staff to plan a cross-Channel operation and British Lt-Gen Sir Frederick Morgan was designated COSSAC—Chief of Staff to Supreme Allied Commander (Designate). In May 1943 at the Washington Trident Conference it was formally agreed that this operation, now codenamed Overlord, would take place on May 1, 1944, and this date was confirmed at the subsequent Quadrant conference in Quebec, the Americans overruling Churchill's proposals for an alternative offensive through Italy and the Balkans. Even so preparations proceeded at a desultory pace as Churchill still harbored thoughts of an alternative strategy as late as December 1943.

At that point the die was cast by the choice of the American Gen Dwight D. Eisenhower as Supreme Commander Allied Expeditionary Force. He immediately absorbed the COSSAC staff into an organization known as Supreme Headquarters Allied Expeditionary- Force (SHAEF) based at Norfolk House, St James Square, London. At the beginning of 1944 over 1,100 British and American officers and other ranks were working at SHAEF and this number would increase in the months ahead.

Eisenhower was aged 53 at the time of his appointment as Supreme Commander and as a brigadier- general he had worked on the early plans for Operation Roundup. He was noted for his personal charm and ability to work with allied leaders and commanders, and this made him a natural choice as the C–in–C for the invasion of North Africa. It was he who had the idea to set up a fully integrated Anglo- American staff at all levels and the success of this led to its adoption for all future allied operations including Overlord. With an American as the Supreme Commander, the subsidiary commands went to British officers. ACM Tedder was nominated as Eisenhower's Deputy Supreme Com- mander while ACM Leigh-Mallory was C–in–C of the Allied Air Forces. Adm Sir Bertram Ramsay, RN was in command of the naval forces and responsible for the actual cross-Channel naval operation codenamed Operation

Neptune. Ramsay was an officer of enormous experience and, indeed, had directed the evacuation at Dunkirk (Operation Dynamo) before planning and commanding the landings in North Africa and Sicily. His role in the success of the Normandy landings cannot be overstated, but unfortunately he was killed in an air crash in January 1945. Finally, the Supreme Ground Force Commander was Gen Sir Bernard Montgomery, already famous for his victory at El Alamein; subsequently, he would lead the British 21st Army Group onward from Normandy to the plains of Northern Germany where he accepted the German surrender on the Lüneburger Heide (Lunenburg Heath) on May 4, 1945.

That final moment was almost 18 months away when Montgomery took up his appointment at SHAEF. By that time the site of the landings had already been decided as the Baie de la Seine between the River Orne and Caen on the east side, and the base of Cotentin Peninsula in the west. Other sites had been investigated, notably the Pas de Calais, but the Normandy area was less strongly defended and offered better terrain for post invasion expansion of the beachhead, including the construction of airfields. Nevertheless, Montgomery was instrumental in persuading Eisenhower that the original COSSAC plan for an initial landing by three divisions supported by elements of one airborne division was quite insufficient and ran the risk of being repulsed. Consequently it was agreed that the initial force would comprise five divisions with another two available for an immediate follow up, while three full airborne divisions

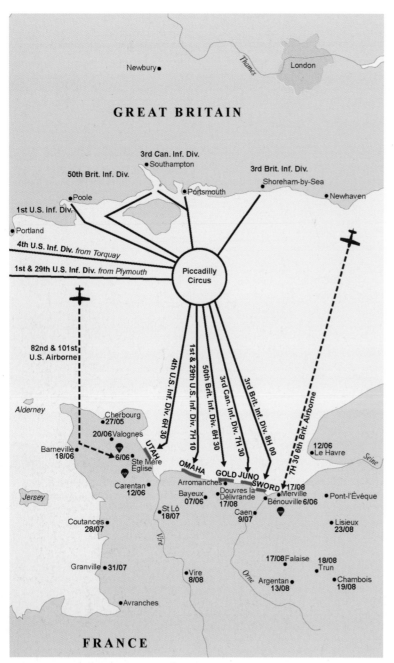

GREAT BRITAIN

Newbury

London

Thames

3rd Can. Inf. Div.
Southampton

50th Brit. Inf. Div.

3rd Brit. Inf. Div.
Shoreham-by-Sea

Poole

Portsmouth

Newhaven

1st U.S. Inf. Div.

Portland

4th U.S. Inf. Div. *from Torquay*

1st & 29th U.S. Inf. Div. *from Plymouth*

Piccadilly
Circus

82nd & 101st
U.S. Airborne

Alderney

Cherbourg
27/05

20/06 Valognes

Barneville
18/06

6/06

Ste Mère
Eglise

UTAH

4th U.S. Inf. Div. 6H 30

1st & 29th U.S. Inf. Div. 7H 10

50th Brit. Inf. Div. 6H 30

3rd Can. Inf. Div. 7H 30

3rd Brit. Inf. Div. 8H 00

7H 30 6th Brit. Airborne

OMAHA

GOLD JUNO

SWORD 17/08

Arromanches

Bayeux
07/06

Douvres la
Délivrande
17/08

Merville

Bénouville 6/06

12/06
Le Havre

Seine

Pont-l'Évêque

Jersey

Carentan
12/06

St Lô
18/07

Caen
9/07

Lisieux
23/08

Coutances
28/07

Vire

17/08 Falaise

18/08
Trun

Granville 31/07

Vire
8/08

Orne

Argentan
13/08

Chambois
19/08

Avranches

FRANCE

Above: *The assault plan—to the west, the First US Army, landing VII Corps on Utah and V Corps on Omaha; to the east, the Second BR Army, landing XXX Corps on Gold and I Corps on Juno and Sword. The flanks were covered by airborne divisions, the US 82nd and 101st in the west; the British 6th Airborne in the east.*

Opposite, above: *The strategic plan—as is always the case, the tactical eventualities didn't match it. The breakout took longer than expected, but Paris was, nevertheless, liberated on August 25 (D+80), ahead of this schedule.*

14

would be deployed on the flanks. These changes required time to implement and consequently it was agreed that Overlord would be postponed by one month to the beginning of June 1944. Investigations of factors such as tides and state of the moon led to the selection of June 5 as the target date —D-Day.

In its final form, the assault planned to land three divisions of the British Second Army on three beach areas in the eastern sector, while two divisions of the First US Army would land on two beaches in the western sector. Prior to the actual landings, the eastern flank of the British beach areas would be secured by troops of the 6th Airborne Division, particularly tasked with securing the vital Orne river crossing at Bénouville. In the American sector troops of the 82nd and 101st Airborne Divisions would land at Ste Mère Église and Carentan to disrupt German movements in the Contentin peninsula. On the naval side the Eastern Task Force would be commanded by Rear Adm Sir Philip Vian, RN and the Western Task Force by Rear Adm A.G. Kirk, USN. One of the reasons for the postponement of the original D-Day date was a severe shortage of specialized amphibious warfare vessels, particularly the vital LSTs. This was partly due to the priority accorded in 1943 to the construction of anti-submarine escorts, but also to the fact that as an extension of the Mediterranean strategy, a large-scale landing (Operation Dragoon) in the south of France was planned as an immediate followup to Overlord in the north. It quickly became apparent that there were not enough LSTs to support both of these operations and eventually Dragoon was postponed until August 1944 and the necessary LSTs were reallocated.

By the end of May 1944 the south coast of England was crowded with thousands of troops and their vehicles and equipment. Many of them were hard at work waterproofing their vehicles and equipment. Whole areas were sealed off from civilian access and every port, harbor, inlet, and estuary was occupied by lines of landing craft and their naval escorts. Tension rose as all the months of training in preparation for the landings reached a climax on May 25 when all holders of the operation orders were permitted to open them. Three days later, the date of June 5 was promulgated and from that time onward a blanket of security was imposed on all soldiers, sailors, and airmen. Embarked troops were confined to their ships and all normal mail and telephone communications halted.

Unfortunately at this point nature took a hand and a considerable deterioration in the weather conditions occurred. After extensive discussion and advice from meteorologists, as well as his military and naval staffs, Eisenhower took the momentous decision on the evening of Saturday, June 3, to postpone Overlord for 24 hours. This was the latest time at which a postponement could be effected as some of the convoys and support vessels,

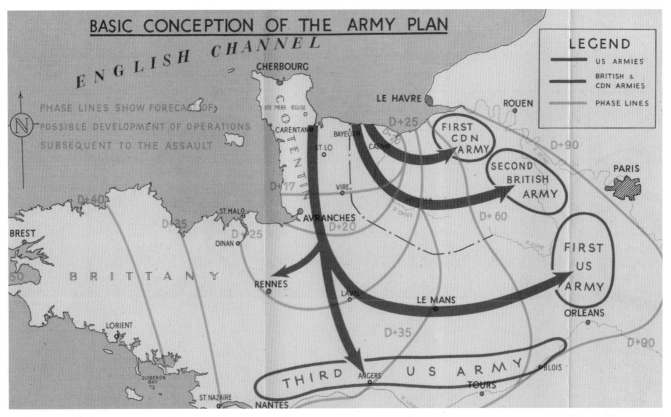

BASIC CONCEPTION OF THE ARMY PLAN

ENGLISH CHANNEL

PHASE LINES SHOW FORECAST OF
POSSIBLE DEVELOPMENT OF OPERATIONS
SUBSEQUENT TO THE ASSAULT

LEGEND
— US ARMIES
— BRITISH & CDN ARMIES
— PHASE LINES

CHERBOURG · LE HAVRE · ROUEN · PARIS
STE MERE EGLISE
CARENTAN · BAYEUX · CAEN
ST LO
FIRST CDN ARMY
SECOND BRITISH ARMY
VIRE
AVRANCHES D+20
ST MALO
BREST
DINAN
BRITTANY
RENNES
LAVAL
LE MANS
FIRST US ARMY
ORLEANS
LORIENT
THIRD US ARMY
QUIBERON BAY
BLOIS
TOURS
ST NAZAIRE
NANTES
ANGERS

ENEMY ORDER OF BATTLE IN THE WEST AS AT 6 JUNE, 1944.

LEGEND
Panzer:
□ PANZER .... 9 } 10
○ PANZER GRENADIER ..1
Infantry:
▨ FIELD 17
▨ LOWER ESTABLISHMENT..24 } 48
○ TRAINING 7
TOTAL 58

FIFTEENTH ARMY

SEVENTH ARMY

FIRST ARMY

NINETEENTH ARMY

Left: *The opposition—with Fifteenth Army massed opposite Patton in the Pas de Calais, it's easy to see why the subterfuge was so important. The Official British History estimates 156,115 men landed on D-Day: 57,500 Americans and 75,215 British and Canadians from the sea; 15,500 Americans and 7,900 British from the air. The Germans had 46 infantry and 9 tank divisions in France, but many of them were too far from the action to be involved as the bridgehead was created.*

The key German units on the spot defending against the landings were:

• *716th Inf Div (Static) on the British and Canadian beaches. This division included those not up to the Eastern Front for medical reasons, "Hiwis" (Soviet PoWs), and conscripts from occupied countries.*

• *352nd Inf Div between Bayeux and Carentan, covering the Omaha sector, was composed of experienced troops.*

• *91st Air Landing Div in the Cotentin Peninsula was also a strong unit and included the 6th Fallschirmjäger (Parachute) Regt.*

• *709th Inf Div (Static) on the east and north of the Cotentin defending Utah, was also equipped with a number of the conscripted "Ost" battalions (see page 92).*

Right: *The south of England was full of men, vehicles, and materiels, all following carefully organized flow plans to ensure they embarked on time. The logistical exercise was remarkable. Here, a Sherman BARV passes Shermans of the 13th/18th Royal Hussars during the regiment's move from Petworth to its embarkation point at Gosport, June 2.*

Opposite, above: *A well-known photograph, but an evocative one. Ike talks to Lt Wallace C. Strobel of Company E, 502nd PIR during a walkabout following the inspection of 101st AB Div at Greenham Common on June 5. Behind Ike, in British service dress, is Lt-Col Jim Gault, Eisenhower's aide.*

Opposite, below: *With the silhouette of Brunel's unmistakable Royal Albert Bridge spanning the River Tamar at Plymouth in the background, landing craft ferry troops out to the waiting ships preparatory to crossing the Channel.*

especially those based in Northern Ireland, had already sailed and these had to be recalled. Despite the postponement, there was still no guarantee that the weather conditions would be suitable on the 6th and it was not until late on the evening of Sunday, June 4, that the final "Go" decision was made. Even then a recall might have been possible, but on the Monday morning it was clear that a reasonable break in the weather would occur and everyone moved into high gear as the great enterprise got underway. Strangely enough, on the German side meteorologists had also been monitoring the weather and had decided that any invasion attempt was unlikely over the next few days. Because of this both Rommel and the German naval commander, Adm Krancke, decided that it was an ideal opportunity to get away for a few days.

During the night of June 5/6, 1944, the sky resounded to the throbbing sound of aero engines as the great aerial armada carrying British, Canadian, and American paratroopers set off across the Channel. In the early hours of the morning, while it was still dark, they began to touch down in France, the first of over 150,00 allied troops to land in Normandy. At sea, the massive fleet consisted of no fewer than 1,213 warships (including 5 battleships, 2 monitors, and 23 cruisers for bombardment duties) escorting a total of 2,468 landing ships and craft which crossed the Channel under their own power. In addition, there were another 1,656 smaller landing craft, barges, and ferries, most of which were transported to the beach-offloading areas in larger vessels. The assault plan called for the first troops to land in the American (western) sector from 06:30 onward, with the eastern sector progressively later due to tidal differences. The last initial landing was to occur around 07:45.

Despite the magnitude of the operation, and the effect of weather and postponements, it is remarkable to be able to record that after all the years, months, and weeks of planning, the landings on D-Day, June 6, were an outstanding success. As will be told in this book, there were, of course, some errors, setbacks, even disasters, but at the end of that momentous day Allied troops were, at last, ashore in north-west Europe and were there to stay.

Above: *The Germans had put a lot of thought into beach defenses, which ranged from defenses to stop landing craft reaching the beach—such as Belgian gates, designed to rip the bottom from landing craft, and mines—through to the network of Widerstandsnester ("resistance nests") and artillery batteries.*

Below: *There were many different types of emplacement on the Atlantic Wall. This one, number 669 of the Regelbau (standard build) system, was designed to give a 60-degree arc of fire. It was used for field guns with calibers from 75mm to 155mm and examples can be found at Merville and St. Martin.*

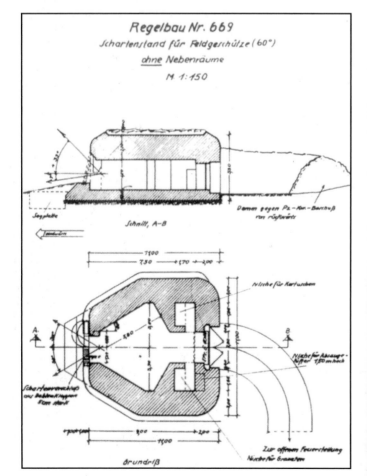

The Atlantic Wall

The Germans had a long time to prepare for the Allied landings. Having taken Europe by storm in 1939–41, they started to fortify a border that stretched from the Arctic Circle to the Pyrenees after the St. Nazaire Raid. Hitler's March 23, 1942, *Führerdirectiv* 40 ordered the construction of major defenses and involved Organization Todt—the slave labor organization named after its founder Fritz Todt, although Albert Speer ran it after Todt's death in 1942. The key areas—north France and the Channel Islands, in particular—saw significant work, much of it by PoWs and laborers conscripted from conquered lands. At its peak it employed 1.4 million people in what were, effectively, conditions of slave labor, and many of those involved did not survive.

Below: *Nullifying the coastal batteries was critical to the success of Overlord. This map shows the location of batteries in the landing area. They were pummeled by aerial bombardment before the invasion and by the naval task forces during the event. The Merville Battery was taken out by British airborne troops, and that at Pointe du Hoc was attacked by US Rangers. The interdiction was successful and the batteries did not affect the outcome of the battle.*

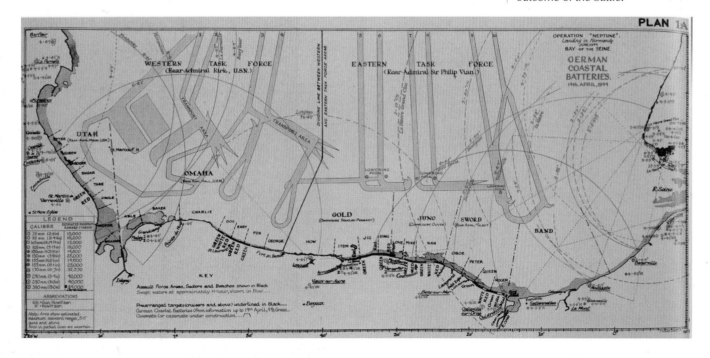

Right and Below: *The German beach defenses were designed to impede landing craft and there were many of them. The landings in North Africa and Italy had shown the Allies the need for forces to prepare the way for the assault troops and for strong beach parties to land with the first waves to organize the landings: mark limits with flags (or lights at night), identify safe exits, control incoming craft, and communicate with the naval forces. On the British beaches these tasks fell to the RM Beachhead Commandos. With the confusion of the first landings—the problems caused by the beach defenses, enemy counterattacks, mortar and artillery fire, and snipers, these beach parties had an almost impossible job which they fulfilled with great bravery.*

Right: *A number of tank turrets were emplaced along the coast, often from older French Renault models. This one, photographed on Omaha Beach, came from the Henschel VK 3001H medium tank program.*

Right: *Rommel's defensive doctrine was to stop any enemy at the coast. When he arrived in Normandy he was dismayed at the number of unfinished defenses and the slow pace of construction. He worked hard to create a strong defense with interlinked hardpoints, extensive beach defenses, massive numbers of mines, inundation of low-lying areas and filling potential landing areas with wooden posts—"Rommel's asparagus." He argued that the armor reserve should be close enough to the coast to be used to push the invaders back before they gained a foothold. Von Rundstedt, Guderian, and the commander of Panzer Gruppe West, Leo Geyr, didn't agree. They felt that the tanks should be held away from the coast and should engage the enemy as he moved inland. In the end, Allied air supremacy, helped by the RAF attack on Leo Geyr's HQ (see page 35), ensured that the Panzers weren't able to fulfill either strategy.*

Below: *Heavily camouflaged Jagdpanzer IV of 116th Panzer Division rushes to the front. Attrition by "Jabos," Allied fighter-bombers, meant that this journey was fraught with danger.*

Bottom: *The battery at Longues (see page 144).*

CHAPTER 1
PREPARATIONS

Troops await their turn to embark in Plymouth on the hardstanding used today for the Torpoint Ferry. The warship in the right background is USS Augusta, flagship for the Western Task Force. This Northampton class heavy cruiser was used as a presidential flagship and carried both Franklin D. Roosevelt and Harry S. Truman. Augusta left Plymouth on June 5 with Lt-Gen Omar Bradley and his staff on board. They would finally disembark and set up on French soil on June 10.

"The ardor and spirit of the troops, as I saw myself, embarking in these last few days was splendid to witness. Nothing that equipment, science or forethought could do has been neglected, and the whole process of opening this great new front will be pursued with the utmost resolution both by the commanders and by the United States and British Governments whom they serve."

Prime Minister Winston Churchill's House of Commons address given on June 6, 1944

The text on the monument reads:

'D' DAY EMBARKATION RAMPS
BEACON QUAY

BUILT MAY 30th 1943 .... FOR JUNE 6th 1944

FOR "D" DAY OPERATION OVERLORD .... ONTO MULBERRY HARBOUR, CAEN AND BERLIN.

ROYAL ENGINEERS "THE ENABLERS" 935 PORT CONSTRUCTION AND REPAIR COMPANY.

Above: *The Torquay Slipways D-Day Embarkation Hards. As the panels explain, 68 hards were built between Falmouth and Felixstowe in 1942–43 providing berths for LCTs and LSTs. Those at Torquay were unusually steeply inclined, supported by reinforced concrete frameworks. The hards were operated by a dedicated detachment. Core personnel included a Commanding Hardmaster and Embarkation Staff Officers who would over-see loading, a maintenance and repair crew, which would expand to 40 men when in operational use. Where the hards were used exclusively by American troops, the US forces provided crews.*

Right: *An AA halftrack backs toward LST 47. The next time it will see dry land is on Utah's Tare Green Beach. In the back-ground, Dartmouth in Devon.*

Any great military operation requires a degree of surprise in order to achieve its objectives. In the case of a cross-Channel invasion of the French coast this was almost impossible, as the German high command was well aware that such an operation was imminent and had taken substantial steps ensure that it would not succeed. These included the costruction of formidable fixed defenses along the Channel coast, especially around ports such as Dieppe, Le Havre, and Cherbourg, and the erection of numerous obstructions and booby traps on the various beaches where a landing might occur. German forces in France and the Low Countries were under the command of Field Marshal von Rundstedt as Commander-

in-Chief West and along the Channel coast of France, Belgium, and Holland was Army Group B commanded by the famous Field Marshal Erwin Rommel. Among the troops under his command was the Seventh Army, which covered Normandy and Brittany, and the Fifteenth Army covering the Pas de Calais and Flanders. At the time of the landings on June 6 there were four infantry divisions (352, 709, 711, and 716) covering the coast from Cherbourg to Honfleur and they were supported by a single Panzer division (21st Pz Div) although two more (12th SS "Hitlerjugend" and 116th Pz Div) were held further inland as a mobile reserve. A much greater concentration of infantry divisions was positioned around the Pas de Calais, although again supported by a single Panzer division.

The disposition of these forces demonstrated the uncertainty in German minds as to where the invasion would occur. Although it was impossible to hide the massive build up of forces in the UK, considerable effort was put into misleading the Germans as to the exact objectives under a scheme known as Plan Fortitude. This had several elements including the establishment of several fake Army units (notably the so-called First US Army Group led by General Patton) with dummy headquarters generating a stream of radio traffic which was intercepted by the Germans, and ensuring that a network of double agents fed back more false information. The general picture presented to the Germans was that the main invasion would take place at the Pas de Calais and any Normandy landings would be an elaborate diversion. In addition it was hinted that further landings of troops shipped directly from America would occur on the Biscay coast. These and other schemes were intended not only to deceive the Germans as to where the main landing would occur but also to keep them guessing even after the allies were establishing the Normandy beachhead.

In the event these schemes proved to be outstandingly successful. When the Seventh and Fifteenth Army headquarters received the initial reports of airborne landings early on June 6, these were dismissed as diversionary operations and when dawn broke and the whole invasion armada was visible there was still a groundswell of opinion that this was diversionary operation. This view was reinforced by the staging of a false invasion fleet across the Channel towards the Pas de Calais. Although a few surface craft were involved, the appearance of a mass of shipping on German radar screens was the result of formations of allied bombers (including No 617 Squadron, the Dambusters) flying extremely accurate flight patterns and dropping foil strips (Window) at precise points to produce the illusion of a fleet advancing steadily at 8 knots. When dawn broke the alerted defences in that area were mystified when no ships were visible. Perhaps the person most taken in by these deception measures was Hitler himself who for two vital days refused

Top: *In May 1944, the dress rehearsal for Operation Neptune took place: Exercise Fabius, six separate exercises to rehearse every possible aspect of the invasion. Here, infantrymen of the 1st Bn, Canadian Scottish Regiment, take up positions in an LCA from LSI(M) HMS Queen Emma.*

Above: *Two snipers of the 1st Canadian Parachute Bn during an inspection by King George VI, Queen Elizabeth, and Princess Elizabeth, on Salisbury Plain, May 17. The snipers wear "ghillie" camouflage suits.*

Left: *5th Rangers load onto LCAs in Weymouth harbor before making their way to HMS Prince Baudouin for transit across to Omaha. Originally built in 1933–34 for Belgian State Railways, she was converted to a landing vessel in January 1943.*

THIS·MEMORIAL·
WAS·PRESENTED·BY·THE·
UNITED·STATES·ARMY·
AUTHORITIES·TO·THE·
PEOPLE·OF·THE·SOUTH·
HAMS·WHO·GENEROUSLY·
LEFT·THEIR·HOMES·AND·
THEIR·LANDS·TO·PROVIDE·
A·BATTLE·PRACTICE·AREA·
FOR·THE·SUCCESSFUL·
ASSAULT·IN·NORMANDY·
·IN·JUNE·1944·
THEIR·ACTION·RESULTED·
IN·THE·SAVING·OF·MANY·
HUNDREDS·OF·LIVES·AND·
CONTRIBUTED·IN·NO·SMALL·
MEASURE·TO·THE·SUCCESS·
·OF·THE·OPERATION·
THE·AREA·INCLUDED·THE·
VILLAGES·OF·BLACKAWTON·
·CHILLINGTON·
EAST·ALLINGTON·SHERFORD·
SLAPTON·STOKENHAM·
STRETE·AND·TORCROSS·
TOGETHER·WITH·MANY·
OUTLYING·FARMS·HOUSES

Slapton in Devon was requisitioned by the British Government in late 1943 for use by US forces destined to land on Utah Beach, which Slapton Sands closely resembled. The inhabitants were evacuated (top) at short notice and the US personnel moved in. The US Army later presented a memorial to thank the people of Slapton (right and A in aerial photo). On April 22–28, 1944, Exercise Tiger took place, and during the night of April 27 a convoy of poorly protected LSTs was attacked by E-boats leading to some 1,000 casualties. Forty years later, after tireless work by Ken Small, the full story was told. This M4 (above and B in aerial photo above left) was recovered from the sea and placed at Slapton as a memorial to those who died. The exercise pictured (left) is on Slapton Sands and shows Coast Guard-manned LCI(L)-85 which would be so severely damaged by enemy fire during the invasion that it sank later on D-Day. (See also photo page 118.)

Above: *Embarkation. Rangers of the 2nd Battalion on the seafront at Weymouth. They embarked on June 1 and so spent five days on board before D-Day. Some carry Bangalore torpedoes; some wear green assault vests.*

Opposite, above and center left/right: *In Devon, at Countess Wear outside Exeter, the River Exe and the 16th century Exeter Ship Canal are in a similar configuration to the River Orne and Canal de Caen at Bénouville—today known as Pegasus and Horsa bridges (see pages 70–73). As the plaque on the Exeter Canal bridge identifies (****Opposite, center right***), "In May 1944, these bridges played an important part in the preparations for D-Day. They were used over a period of three days and nights, for rehearsals of the famous and crucial glider borne attack on the bridge over the Canal de Caen (Pegasus Bridge) and the River Orne (Horsa Bridge), by the Second Battalion Oxford-shire and Buckinghamshire Light Infantry, on the night 5/6 June 1944."*

Opposite, below: *The marshaling areas for assault and follow-up forces.*

to release the 12th and 116th Panzer Divisions for action against the Allied beachhead in Normandy, convinced that further landings in the Pas de Calais were to follow. Amazingly, elements of Plan Fortitude continued to operate as late as the end of August by which time Paris had been liberated and allied troops were advancing well into Northern France.

The main reason why the landings in France were not possible until summer 1944 was the time taken to assemble, equip, and train the forces involved. As well as the five divisions and supporting troops to be landed on D-Day, Montgomery's 21st Army Group included 13 divisions comprising the First US Army and a similar number making up the British Second Army. In addition there was the First Canadian Army and various airborne troops as well as the Polish Armored Division. Almost all of these would be landed in Normandy in the two weeks after D-Day. However, prior to that date all of the US and Canadian troops needed to be carried across that Atlantic, assigned accommodation areas in the UK, and be put through a rigorous training program alongside their British comrades. A significant number of troops crossed the Atlantic in the great liners *Queen Mary* and *Queen Elizabeth*, each of which could carry a whole division in a single crossing.

The whole of the south of England and South Wales became a huge encampment with men, vehicles, and equipment to found at every turn. The British and Canadian troops who would be landing on the eastern Normandy beaches were billeted throughout south-east England and the Home Counties and would sail from ports such as Southampton, Portsmouth, Shoreham, and Newhaven. To the west the US divisions were billeted in Dorset, Somerset, Devon, and Cornwall with access to ports at Portland, Weymouth, Torbay, Dartmouth, Plymouth, and Falmouth. Follow-up troops of the British I and XXX Corps were based even further afield in East Anglia and would embark in the Thames estuary and at Felixstowe while US follow-up troops including the 2nd and 90th Infantry Divisions were based in South Wales using Swansea and Cardiff for embarkation.

Much to the chagrin of the units involved, those divisions which had recent battle experience were selected to be among the first to land and these included the British 50th Inf Div and the US 1st Inf Div both of which had already fought in North Africa and Sicily. However, many of the other units lacked battle experience and the one-month postponement from May to June provided vitally needed time to carry out additional training. In early May a full-scale rehearsal codenamed Operation Fabius was carried out at beaches along the south coast including Slapton Sands in South Devon. The latter area had been requisitioned in December 1943 as a training area for US troops and the whole civilian population had been evacuated so that realistic training, including live firing, could take place. It was here that another training exercise, Operation Tiger, which involved troops bound for Utah beach, took place during the last week of April 1944 with tragic results. Due to various misunderstandings and poor communications a force of nine German E-boats was able to attack one of the troop convoys in Lyme Bay on the night of April 27/28. Three LSTs were sunk or badly damaged and nearly 1,000 US soldiers and sailors were lost. Ironically this was well in excess of the actual casualties sustained by this force on D-Day itself. Fortunately this was the only serious incident of this nature and by the beginning of June the Allied forces were as ready as they would ever be and waited impatiently for the off.

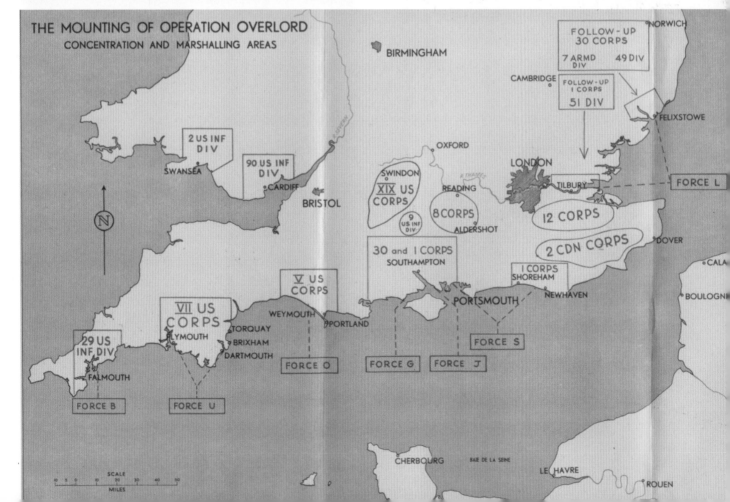

THE MOUNTING OF OPERATION OVERLORD
CONCENTRATION AND MARSHALLING AREAS

Armor was an important component of the seaborne assault, necessary to support the infantry against the beach defenses housed in hardened emplacements. At the least, these tanks had to be waterproofed and provided with wading equipment (as shown at left). Additionally, serious thought had gone into the beachhead requirements and this had led to various novelties, such as the Duplex Drive (DD) Shermans (this page) which employed a canvas structure and propellers to allow them to swim. Other "funnies" included flail tanks (**opposite, centre left and right**) used against minefields or beach defenses rigged with explosives, and the AVRE (armored vehicle Royal Engineers) armed with a bunker-busting externally loaded spigot mortar that fired an HE projectile some 150 yards. This one (**opposite, bottom**) can be seen outside Lion-sur-Mer. The waterproofing of the tanks was a long and boring process that required the outside of the tank to be wire-brushed and "all nuts and bolts, openings, escape hatches and gun ports were sealed and made waterproof"as Jim Ramsey, gunner in a flail tank of A Squadron Westminster Dragoons remembered in a BBC interview in 2004. The exhaust had extensions fitted to allow the tanks to operate in turret-deep water. "To make the hatches waterproof," Jack Tear of the Royal Marine Armoured Support Regiment remembered, "long candles of soft sealing asbestos was put around the edges by our ammunition squad and this worked fine."

CHAPTER 2
AIRPOWER

The Republic P-47 Thunderbolt was a hugely successful fighter-bomber. Over 15,000 of all versions of the P-47 were built and it continued in service into the 1960s. This example wears the colors of 84th Fighter Squadron P-47D 42-74742 Snafu, the aircraft of Lt Severino B. Calderon in late 1944 and bears invasion stripes—the alternating three white and two black bands used as a recognition aid. In reality it is a P-47G, one of around 350 built by Curtiss in Buffalo, NY in 1944 and used for training stateside.

"The enemy's air superiority has a very grave effect on our movements. There's simply no answer to it."
Rommel, when he was commander of German Army Group B in Normandy, days before he was strafed off the road by Spitfires and seriously injured

Although Overlord required the deployment of an immense naval armada, the operation could not have been carried out as successfully without the Allies complete command of the air. The Air Commander-in-Chief, AEAF, was Air Chief Marshal Sir Trafford Leigh-Mallory whose headquarters were at Uxbridge. Under his direct command were the US Ninth Air Force and the British Second Tactical Air Force which were tasked with direct support of the invasion fleet and of ground troops once ashore. In addition the ADGB fighter groups came under his control and played a prominent part in covering the covering the invasion fleet and its various embarkation ports. Despite the objections of their respective commanders (Air Marshal Harris and General Carl Spaatz) the RAF's Bomber Command and US Eighth Air Force heavy bomber squadrons were diverted from their strategic campaign against Germany to the support of Overlord Operations from mid-April until September 1944. Finally, there were the transport and glider squadrons needed to carry the airborne forces into action and these comprised the US IXth Troop Carrier Command and RAF 38 and 46 Groups. In total these forces totaled 5,886 front-line combat aircraft made up of 2,190 heavy bombers, 744 light and medium bombers, and 2,952 fighters. To these figures must be added 1,100 transport aircraft and glider tugs.

Allied estimates credited the German air forces available to operate against Overlord operations with some 330 bombers and reconnaissance aircraft and 260 fighters. The overwhelming strength of the Allied air forces was further emphasized by the fact that they flew approximately 14,000 sorties on D-Day while the Luftwaffe managed only 300 and very few of these actually made a successful attack. One reason for the weak strength of the Luftwaffe was the three-month aerial campaign preceding Overlord which had the objective of destroying the German transportation system so that their ability to move reinforcements and mount counterattacks would be severely restricted. The so-called Transportation Plan was the brainchild of Professor Zuckerman, one of Churchill's scientific advisors, who pinpointed the significant targets whose destruction would cause the maximum disruption. The campaign was extremely successful, destroying 75% of railway rolling stock within 150 miles of the Normandy beaches, completely dislocating the railway system throughout north-west Europe, and destroying virtually every road and rail bridge accessing the battle zone. A side effect of this campaign was the destruction of almost 5,000 enemy aircraft and it was this that reduced the Luftwaffe response to a token effort.

On D-Day the assault beaches were under fighter protection provided by six squadrons of RAF Spitfires at low level and three squadrons of Ninth Air Force P-47 Thunderbolts at high level, these squadrons being relieved at regular intervals to maintain continuous cover. In addition four squadrons of P-38 Lightnings were maintained over the shipping lanes and assembly areas.

Top: *The P-51, engined with the Packard V-1650-7—a licence-built Rolls-Royce Merlin 60—was the best long-range fighter of the war. Here, in Normandy, P-51D Fool's Paradise IV flown by Evan M "Mac" McCall.*

Opposite, top: *The C-47 (the Dakota in British and Common-wealth service) was the Allied workhorse and used in many roles from VIP transport to glider-tower.*

Opposite, center: *Refueling and rearming P-47s on one of the airstrips constructed once the bridgehead was secured.*

Opposite, below: *The RAF's fighter-bomber of choice was the Hawker Typhoon. This one, Pulverizer IV, was flown by Harry Hardy of No 440 Sqn, RCAF and is pictured at Eind-hoven, Holland in 1945. The RAF Typhoons and Tempests carried bombs or RP-3 three-inch rockets armed with either 60lb HE or 25lb AP heads (inset). In one of the most successful tactical uses of Ultra intelligence, on June 10, only hours after decrypting the signals traffic, rocket-armed Typhoons and Mitchell bombers of the RAF's 2TAF attacked Gen Leo Geyr von Schweppenburg's Panzer Group West's HQ at La Caine. As well as destroying the signals equipment, it killed 17 officers including chief of staff Maj-Gen Sigismund-Helmut von Dawans, and wounded von Schweppenburg. The Germans lost their only organization in the west capable of handling numbers of mobile divisions.*

RAF Mosquito nightfighter squadrons were available to cover the the hours of darkness and although central control of both day and nightfighters was exercised from Uxbridge, three FDTs were deployed to provide a degree of local control, particularly for the nightfighters.

During the actual assault heavy bombers were used in an effort to neutralize the defenses but the results were not always satisfactory. On Omaha a force of Eighth Air Force B-17s was tasked with carpet-bombing the defenses at the top of the beach as the troops landed. As they flew in over the beach a natural desire to avoid hitting their own men led to a few seconds' delay in releasing bombs with the result that most fell slightly inland where they did little damage. More successful was a subsequent raid a few days later on Le Havre by RAF Lancasters and Mosquitos when over 30 German vessels, including three small destroyers and ten E-boats, were sunk, removing a potential threat to the eastern beaches.

One of the most potent weapons in the allied armory was the RAF's Typhoon fighter-bombers carrying eight 60lb rockets which were particularly effective against tanks and armored vehicles. These were used throughout the Normandy campaign. The American air forces tended to use the P-47 which could carry three 500lb or two 1000lb bombs as a ground-support fighter-bomber. Forward air controllers operating with ground troops were able to call in air support from bomb and rocket armed fighters circling overhead in a "cab rank" system originally developed by the RAF in the North African desert war. This cooperation between ground and air forces took a

Top: *The Allies dropped thousands of pounds of bombs during the run-up to the invasion and after, many of them on towns and cities whose civilian populations had not been evacuated. It is estimated that this bombing caused as many as 50,000 civilian deaths, over 3,000 in Le Havre and 2,000 in Caen alone.*

Above: *The Armstrong Whitworth Albemarle saw use on D-Day when aircraft from Nos 295 and 296 Squadrons towed Horsa and Hamilcar gliders to Normandy.*

Above right: *The Douglas A-20 light bomber was called the Havoc by the USAAF and the Boston by the RAF.*

Right: *The Martin B-26 Marauder was the best medium bomber in the ETO and was used by USAAF, RAF, and SAAF. This is B-26G 44-68219 painted to represent 41-31576 AN-Z* Dinah Might *of the USAAF's 553rd Bomb Squadron. It's on display at the excellent Utah Beach Museum (Musée du Débarquement Utah Beach).*

36

58853 A.

while to become successful, but eventually proved to be a major problem to the Germans.

As soon as the beach bridgehead was established and expanded, engineer battalions began constructing airstrips so that tactical aircraft could operate closer to the front line and transport aircraft could deliver supplies directly into the combat area. The first of these was ready for use in the American sector on the evening of June 8 with others rapidly following. Fewer airfields were established in the British sector due to the slow advance around Caen but those which were available were used by British-based squadrons for rearming and refueling, extending their time over the beachhead.

In the Normandy battles which followed the landings heavy bombers were used on several occasions to blast the German lines before Allied troops commenced an assault while the city of Caen was reduced to rubble in a major attack on June 6/7. Perhaps the ultimate demonstration of Allied air power came in mid-August when the German Seventh Army and Fifth Panzer Army were caught in the Falaise Gap, trapped between British and Canadian forces in the north and Patton's rampaging Third US Army in the south. In perfect flying weather the allied fighter-bombers, particularly the rocket-firing Typhoons, destroyed many vehicles and tanks, taking dreadful toll of the troops attempting to escape on foot to the east. This marked then end of any effective resistance to the Allied breakout from Normandy and the war now moved rapidly north-west into Belgium, Holland, and even Germany itself.

Left and Above: *As soon as they could, the Allies started work on emergency landing strips (ELS), refueling and rearming strips (RRS), and advanced landing grounds (ALG). This is Saint-Pierre-du-Mont above Omaha. Construction began on June 7 and was completed as an ELS by 18:00 on June 8, used primarily by observation aircraft. Rapidly upgraded to become an RRS, by late on June 9 it had become ALG A-1, able to handle aircraft as big as C-47s. A P-38 unit began using the airfield on June 11. The twin-boom Lockheed P-38 Lightning was used to great effect by 370th Fighter Group as a ground-attack aircraft in the Normandy campaign.*

Below left: *The British ALG B-2 at Bazenville would have been completed as the first ALG in Normandy on June 9, but a B-24 Liberator crashlanded there and it took two days to repair the damage. It serviced the first Spitfires of 127 Wing on June 11. This photo shows Typhoon pilots of 121 and 124 Wings discussing operations at Bazenville on June 14. The people have been identified as: in the foreground, on the left, five pilots of No 175 Squadron, RAF including CO, Sqn Ldr M.R. Ingle-Finch (fourth from left); on the right men of No 181 Squadron, RAF including CO, Sqn Ldr Kit North-Lewis sitting on the far right. The farthest group include Wg Cdr C.L. Green (wearing helmet) leader of 121 Wing, and Sqn Ldr W. Pitt-Brown, CO of No 174 Squadron, RAF (on the right, wearing a lanyard). In the back-ground can be seen Spitfire Mk IXs of No 66 Squadron, RAF.*

CHAPTER 3
SEAPOWER

The 14-inch guns of USS Nevada *provided signifi-cant support to the Allies between June 6 and 17. Launched in 1914, USS* Nevada *was the only vessel on Battleship Row to get away during the attack on Pearl Harbor, but had to be beached after being hit by a torpedo and a number of bombs. Refloated and refurbished, she went on to serve with distinction on Atlantic convoys and at the amphibious assaults of Normandy, the south of France, Iwo Jima, and Okinawa. She ended her days in 1948 as a target after enduring the nuclear tests at Bikini.*

"Andrew Higgins is the man who won the war for us. If Higgins had not designed and built those LCVPs (Landing Craft, Vehicle and Personnel), we never could have landed over an open beach. The whole strategy of the war would have been different."

President Dwight D. Eisenhower, 1964 interview

Opposite, top: *HMS* Scylla, *the flagship for Eastern Task Group, was tasked with the bombardment of Ouistreham and provided fire support for the Gold, Sword, and Juno landings. On June 23, she hit a mine and was badly damaged, returning to Spithead under tow.*

Opposite, center: *USS* Augusta *(see also pages 22–23) brought Gen Omar Bradley and his staff to Normandy (they left the ship on the 10th), bombarded ground targets, and anchored off Omaha, provided AA defense, shooting down at least one German aircraft.*

Opposite, below: *The light cruiser* Montcalm *was the second of the six-ship La Galissonniere class. She was one of two French cruisers (the other being the* Georges Leygues*) which were part of Force U off Omaha.*

Below and Bottom: *Ships of the Eastern Task Force sail towards the British and Canadian beaches.*

Apart from the airborne forces landing in advance of the main operation, the conveying of 150,000 men, together with their vehicles and equipment, safely across the English Channel and delivering them onto the Normandy beaches was the responsibility of the Allied naval forces under the command of Adm Sir Bertram Ramsey, RN who was Allied Naval Commander-in-Chief Expeditionary Forces. Inevitably an operation on this scale was going to be an extremely complex affair and there were several factors to be considered. First and foremost was the logistic organizsation to ensure that there were enough transport and assault vessels to carry the landing force and follow-up troops. Each of the five landing beaches was allocated its own convoy, which had then to be escorted by numerous warships to ward off potential air or submarine attacks. One very serious hazard was the existence of extensive German minefields in the Channel and on the approaches to the beaches. Consequently, each convoy was preceded by a flotilla of minesweepers whose task was to clear safe-approach lanes and areas off the beachhead where landing craft could assemble in safety as well as lanes which could be used by supporting warships. Potentially this was one of the most hazardous tasks since, as well as the dangers from the mines themselves, the sweepers had to work close inshore ahead of the first assault waves and consequently could be exposed to heavy fire from German shore batteries. In fact, the leading sweepers were in sight of the Normandy coast on the evening of June 5 but surprisingly there was no German reaction and only one minesweeper (USS *Osprey*) was lost on D-Day itself, although two destroyers were also sunk by mines that day. There were other losses due to mines in the following days but many of these were caused by a new type of German influence mine which were laid at night by aircraft after the invasion had begun.

Each beach was also allocated a force of warships to provide fire support, initially in advance of the landings and then in direct support of the troops ashore. Their targets were mainly known German gun batteries previously located by aerial reconnaissance and subsequently accurate naval gunfire was instrumental in engaging other targets of opportunity and, on several occasions, breaking up German counterattacks. Ships engaged on this task included the battleships HMS *Warspite*, HMS *Ramillies*, USS *Nevada*, USS *Texas*, and USS *Arkansas* as well as the monitors HMS *Roberts* and HMS *Erebus*. Further support was supplied by no fewer than 23 cruisers (including the Free French Navy ships *Montcalm* and *Georges Leygues*) and numerous destroyers, gunboats, and specially adapted landing craft including the LCT(R) which fired spectacular salvos of up to 1,000 5in rockets.

Those ships transporting and supporting the US divisions to Omaha and Utah beaches were designated Force O and Force U respectively and formed the Western Task Force, which also included Force B intended for follow-up operations. This was under the command of Rear Adm A.G.Kirk, USN flying his flag aboard the heavy cruiser USS *Augusta*. Similarly, in the British and Canadian sector the Eastern Task Force, commanded by Rear Adm Sir Philip L.Vian, RN flying his flag aboard the cruiser HMS *Scylla*, comprised Forces S, G, and J intended for Sword, Gold and Juno beaches respectively and a follow-up Force L. As each force approached its allocated beach the transports anchored some 11 miles off the coast and began transferring troops and equipment to ranks of waiting landing craft. Although there were some variations, the basic plan in each case called for an initial landing of tanks supported by gun and rocket-armed landing craft close in to the beachhead. The initial wave of tanks should have consisted of specially adapted amphibious Sherman DD tanks launched some 8,000 yards offshore, but the rough weather conditions made this a hazardous operation so that in some cases the tanks were launched closer in or even landed directly onto the beaches. These were followed by further tanks carried by LCTs which landed at H-hour and one minute later a second wave carried specialized armored

bulldozers and other equipment to clear beach obstacles. On their heels were 20 LCAs carrying the initial wave of assaulting infantry and then over the next two hours successive waves were to bring in the rest of the assault brigade including artillery and other support equipment. A second brigade was then to follow over the next two and a half hours.

There is an old military adage that "no plan survives first contact with the enemy" and this was certainly true on June 6, although the weather and sea conditions caused as many problems as the German forces. Off Omaha the DD tanks experienced the worst conditions and almost all were lost, while even on other beaches wind and tide conspired to cause many assault craft to end up out of position. The results varied from beach to beach but nevertheless, in a retrospective report, Admiral Ramsey was able to say that, "despite the unfavorable weather, in every main essential the plan was carried out as written," a tribute the skill, initiative and perseverance shown by the men of the Allied navies in this great enterprise.

Opposite, clockwise from top:
USCG-20 *was driven ashore during the storm that destroyed the Mulberry A artificial harbor off Omaha. She was repaired and transferred to the Royal Navy (through the WSA) later that year.*

Coast Guard 83-foot cutters USCG-20 *(83401) and* USCG-21 *(83402) off the coast of Normandy. 60 cutters went to England and served as rescue craft off the invasion beaches.*

Auk-class minesweeper USS Tide *(AM-125) sinking off Utah Beach after striking a mine, June 7. USS* PT-509 *and USS* Pheasant *(AM-61) are standing by. The incident was photographed from USS* Threat *(AM-124).*

USS LCI(L)-217, with a barrage balloon in tow, en route for the French coast on June 6.

Taking the wounded back to hospital ships or British near-shore facilities was an important task taken up by a number of specially set-up LSTs. A postwar US Navy Medical Department report emphasized the importance of LSTs in cross-channel evacuation. By D+114 they had carried 41,035 of the casualties for all services (U.S. Navy, 2,433; U.S. Coast Guard, 117; U.S. Army, 41,147; Allies, 1,899; and POWs, 9,101) at an average casualty lift of 123.

Convoy of LCI(L)s en route to the beaches, with barrage balloons overhead, photographed from USS Ancon *(AGC-4) on June 6. Note the 20mm guns on board* Ancon.

Above left: *USS* Arkansas *was launched in 1912. She bombarded German positions around Omaha Beach until June 13, when she was moved to support ground forces in Grandcamp les Bains. On June 25, she bombarded Cherbourg in support of the attack on the port, and subsequently took part in the invasion of the south of France.*

Left: *USS LST-325 (left) and USS LST-388 unloading while stranded at low tide during resupply operations, June 12.*

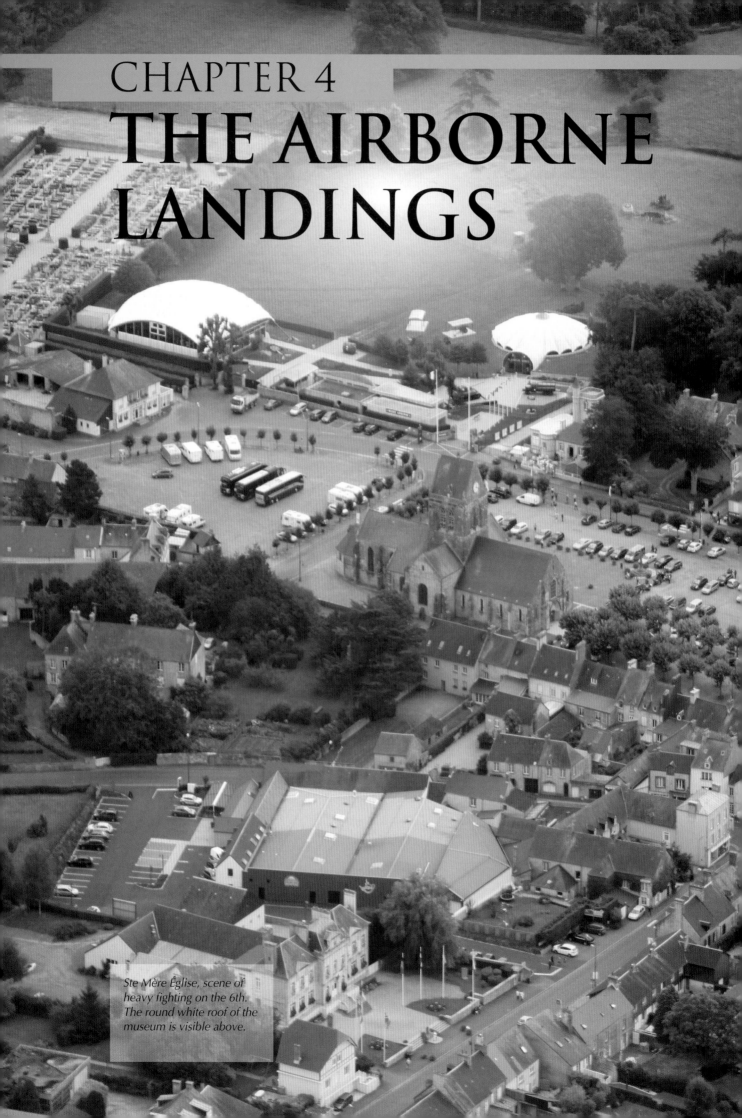

CHAPTER 4
THE AIRBORNE LANDINGS

Ste Mère Église, scene of heavy fighting on the 6th. The round white roof of the museum is visible above.

"Your task will not be an easy one. Your enemy is well-trained, well-equipped and battle-hardened. He will fight savagely."

Dwight D. Eisenhower, address to Allied soldiers on June 6, 1944

Right: *Bob Noody, a bazooka man from Fox Company of 101st Airborne's 506th PIR, waiting for the C-47 to take off on the eve of D-Day. The coils of rope could prove very helpful if you landed in a tree.*
L–R: William G. Olanie, Frank D. Griffin, Robert J. Noody, Lester T. Hegland.

Opposite: *Heavily laden T/4 Joseph Gorenc of 506th PIR climbs into a C-47 on the evening of June 5. Note M1C helmet with chinstrap, Thompson M1 SMG with shoulder sling, M3 trench knife in leg sheath, and reserve parachute in its chest pack.*

46

American Forces

The major tasks facing the American airborne forces were the securing of the causeways leading from the Utah landing beaches and the establishing of a defensive perimeter on the Cotentin peninsula to prevent German forces interfering with the landing operations. For this they had two well-equipped airborne divisions, the 82nd which already had combat experience in North Africa and Sicily, and the 101st which was untried in action. The latter, known as the "Screaming Eagles" and commanded by Gen Maxwell Taylor was allocated three dropping zones (A, C, and D) and two glider landing zones (B and E) in an area between the coast and the main road running north from the town of Carentan to Cherbourg and bounded

Around 13,100 paratroopers of the US 82nd and 101st AB Divs made night drops on June 5/6, followed by 3,937 glider troops flown in during the day. Here, Lt Alex Bobuck (left) and the men of HQ, 3rd Bn, 506th PIR (the "Currahees"), 101st Airborne, are photographed on June 5. In the background is C-47 315087 Lady Lillian from the 440th Troop Carrier Group—not the aircraft from which they will drop. L–R the men are: Pvt Anthony Wincenciak (KIA in Normandy), Sgt Tom Newell (medic; captured but freed on June 8), Pvt Ray Calandrella (captured and PoW until escaped in August 1944), Jesse Cross, John Rinehart (KIA on D-Day), Sgt Bill Pauli (captured but freed on June 8), T/5 Jack Harrison (KIA on D-Day), PFC Harry Howard (captured but freed on June 8), T/5 Charles Riley and S/Sgt John Taormina (captured and PoW until April 1945).

on the south side by the River Douve. Much of the area behind the Utah beaches was flooded marshland and the division's task was to seize and hold the four causeways leading from the beach area inland across the marshes. The 82nd Airborne, led by Gen Matthew Ridgway, was dropped in three zones (O, T, and N plus LZ W) to the west of Ste Mère Église, which they were to occupy and thereby cut road and rail communications to Cherbourg from the south. In addition, they were to secure bridges over the River Merderet to the west of the town to facilitate the advance of US forces across the peninsula with the objective of isolating Cherbourg. This was an important link in Allied strategy as the ultimate capture of Cherbourg would provide a port for the continued build-up of Allied forces after the landings.

The US airborne divisions took off from airfields in the south of England and their route to the dropping zones left the English coast at Portland Bill and then passed to the north and east of the Channel Islands before turning east to cross the west coast of the Cotentin peninsula then across to their dropping zones. As with the British assault, the first troops to drop into France were pathfinders to mark the DZs and glider LZs and set up Eureka Beacons. An hour behind them came an endless armada of 822 twin-engined C-47 transports carrying 13,000 parachute troops of the two divisions. The pathfinder drops were reasonably accurate, although some beacons were set up a mile away from the designated areas. Compared to the British DZs which were reasonably easy to locate as they were just inland from the point at which the coast was crossed on the run in, the American transports had to fly a considerable distance overland to reach their objectives and came under heavy AA fire as they did so. In addition a layer of cloud and fog was forming overland and the combination of this and the AA fire led to several of the aircraft formations breaking up, while the violent maneuvering made it difficult for the heavily laden paratroopers to form up inside the aircraft. The result was that many of the drops were widely scattered although a notable exception was the 316th Group

of the 52nd Troop Carrier Wing which maintained formation throughout the drop and succeeded in putting down elements of the 505th PIR directly onto its designated DZ.

Nevertheless the night developed into a series of actions fought by small groups of paratroopers, often from different units, and it took some time for any sort of command structure to assert itself. This was not helped by the fact that that the Assistant Divisional Commander of the 101st, Brig-Gen Don F. Pratt, was killed when his glider crashed into a tree. The American standard glider was the Waco CG-4 which carried 15 troops compared to 25 aboard the larger British Horsa. Altogether some 2,100 Wacos were available for D-Day operations and although it could carry a jeep as an alternative load, some 300 Horsas in US markings were also used to carry some of the heavier equipment. Items carried by the gliders such as jeeps, artillery, and anti-tank guns were urgently required as soon as the paratroopers could secure the landing zones, but there had been some disagreement among the Allied high command about how this was to be a achieved. AM Leigh-Mallory, the Allied air commander, had serious reservations about the whole operation and forecast unacceptable casualties, but reluctantly agreed to landings at early dawn on the 6th, although the numbers involved were reduced when the extent of German anti-glider obstructions became apparent. Even so, German AA fire took its toll, particularly at LZ W south of Ste Mère Église where German infantry were present in force. In one wave of gliders on the evening of D-Day 64 of a total of 98 were either shot down or destroyed in crash landings, although in most cases the vital equipment they carried was recovered.

Despite these issues the 101st gradually achieved their objectives although the Utah landings ended up further south than their intended touchdown point, with the result that only the two southern causeways were used by the 4th Division to link up with the airborne forces. In the Ste Mère Église area the 82nd was involved in some very fierce fighting, particularly

Above left: *Maj-Gen Matthew B. Ridgway (center), CG 82nd Airborne Division, and staff, overlooking the battlefield near Ribera, Sicily, July 25, 1943. On D-Day he dropped with his troops and fought for the next 33 days advancing to the outskirts of Cherbourg.*

Above: *The "Jumping General"—then Brig-Gen James M. Gavin—lived up to his nickname and jumped into Normandy with 82nd Airborne. He saw a great deal of action as the division fought for the bridges over the Merderet River. When Ridgway was promoted in December 1944, Gavin took command of the 82nd.*

Right: *The Waco CG-4A glider was the mainstay of the US glider troops, and by the end of the war nearly 14,000 had been delivered. It was significantly smaller than the British Horsa (see below) but could land in a smaller location.*

Below right: *Inside, the CG-4A could carry 13 troops and two pilots or some 4,000lb of payload—a jeep or small artillery piece. The men in this photo wear typical glider troops' combat gear—M1 helmets (without the camouflage netting that was used in combat; see photo opposite top) and M41 field jackets—and carry a range of weapons. Most hold the standard Garand M1 rifle although the man at first left has an older Springfield; the man second left carries a Thompson M1 SMG, and next to him there's an M1 bazooka*

Bottom right: *The Airspeed AS.51 Horsa was significantly bigger than the CG-4A and could seat up to 30 men. Over 250 Horsas were used in Battle of Normandy by both the British and US—the USAAF received some 400 during the war.*

Opposite, center: *A wrecked Horsa in Normandy. John C. Warren in his authoritative Airborne Operations of World War II says that 222 Horsa gliders were sent to Normandy, many of which were destroyed in landing accidents or by German fire after landing, although there were only 340 landing casualties. The Waco was easier to handle and sturdier—although US forces had not had much time to train on the British Horsa and Warren identified that the British, dropping the aircraft at a higher altitude and landing in larger fields, achieved good results.*

Left: *American paratrooper James Flanagan of 2nd Pl, C Coy, 502nd PIR holds a Nazi flag captured in a village assault at Marmion Farm, Ravenoville, on June 6. Note, as pointed out on www.battledetective.com, an unusual feature of Pvt James Flanagan is that he is wearing eyeglasses, very rare in US airborne forces. The man to his left isn't carrying a sword. It's a machete. Two types were used: the M1939 22-inch Collins No. 128 and from December 1942 the Army and Marine Corps both adopted the Model 1942—the 18-inch Collins No 37 machete. In an interview published in* World War II *magazine, Flanagan remembered being last out of his aircraft and landing in some four feet of water. He used his cricket clicker (remember the scene in* The Longest Day*?) to join others from the 101st who then attacked and took a German garrison at Ravenoville. The photo was taken after this by a photographer who arrived in a 4th Division jeep from Utah Beach. (See also page 62.) Flanagan took part in the battle for Carentan, and later dropped into Holland as part of Market Garden, where he was wounded. This brave man arrived back at his unit in time to take part in the defense of Bastogne during the Battle of the Bulge.*

Below: *A Waco glider lands.*

around one of the bridges over the Merderet at La Fière and it was several days before the scattered parts of the two divisions were able to form cohesive units as part of the now established VII US Corps which included the 4th Inf Div which had come ashore on D-Day, followed by the 9th Division. The 82nd was instrumental in pushing across the Cotentin peninsula and the west coast was reached on June 14. The 101st was involved in heavy fighting around the town of Carentan until finally relieved on June 27. None of this was achieved without heavy casualties. On D-Day alone each division suffered almost 1,250 men killed or missing and by the time it was withdrawn to England in July the 82nd had a total of 5,245 killed, wounded, or missing. However their actions had secured the flank of the US landings and set the scene for the massive build up of what eventually became Patton's Third US Army which would spectacularly sweep through France and into Germany itself.

Right: *The problems with the drop meant that the US paratroopers were spread thinly over a wide area. This confused the Germans into thinking a larger force had been dropped, but meant that it was difficult to coordinate action allowing the German ground units to put up a strong resistance. Here 82nd Airborne troops in Ste Mère Église.*

Opposite, above: *Some of the fiercest fighting involving 82nd Airborne (shoulder badge inset) was at La Fière, west of Ste Mère Église, a strategic bridge on the Merderet River. Initially taken, German counterattacks drove the defenders from the bridge, but they fought on. The area was finally secured on June 10 by 90th Division.*

Opposite, below left: *Map showing the June 6 airborne assault.*

Opposite, below right: *"Iron Mike"—a replica of Leah Hiebert's "The Airborne Trooper" at Fort Bragg—commemorates the action at La Fière (visible at A in photo above).*

Below: *Sturmgeschütz 40 of StuG Abteilung 1.Kp/Panzerjäger 709 on the RN13 outside Ste Mère Église. It was knocked out on June 7 by the M1 57mm A/Tk gun visible in the background, right, by J. Atchley (he received the DSC for this action) from H Coy, 505th PIR.*

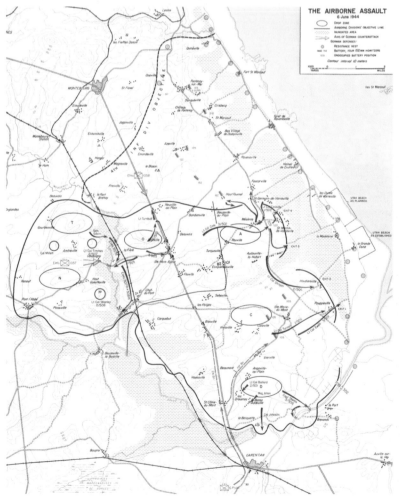

THE AIRBORNE ASSAULT
6 June 1944

Left and Top: *The 101st Airborne's 506th PIR landed on DZ C near the village of Ste Marie du Mont. A group of about a hundred men gathered under Gen Maxwell D.Taylor, who commanded the division, and Lt-Col Julian J. Ewell who commanded 3rd Bn, 506th PIR. They moved toward Utah Beach to take control of the route off the beach. On the way they neutralized a German strongpoint near the town. Another group destroyed a battery west of the town. There was a confused battle in the town itself but on the afternoon of the 6th reinforcements arrived and the town was secured by a group of paras of the 501st and 506th PIR. The water pump is in front of the building identified A (at left) and at A in the two photos above. The war memorial is at B, and road to Utah Beach C.*

Above: *US M8 armored car in the square opposite the church. Note the water pump at left.*

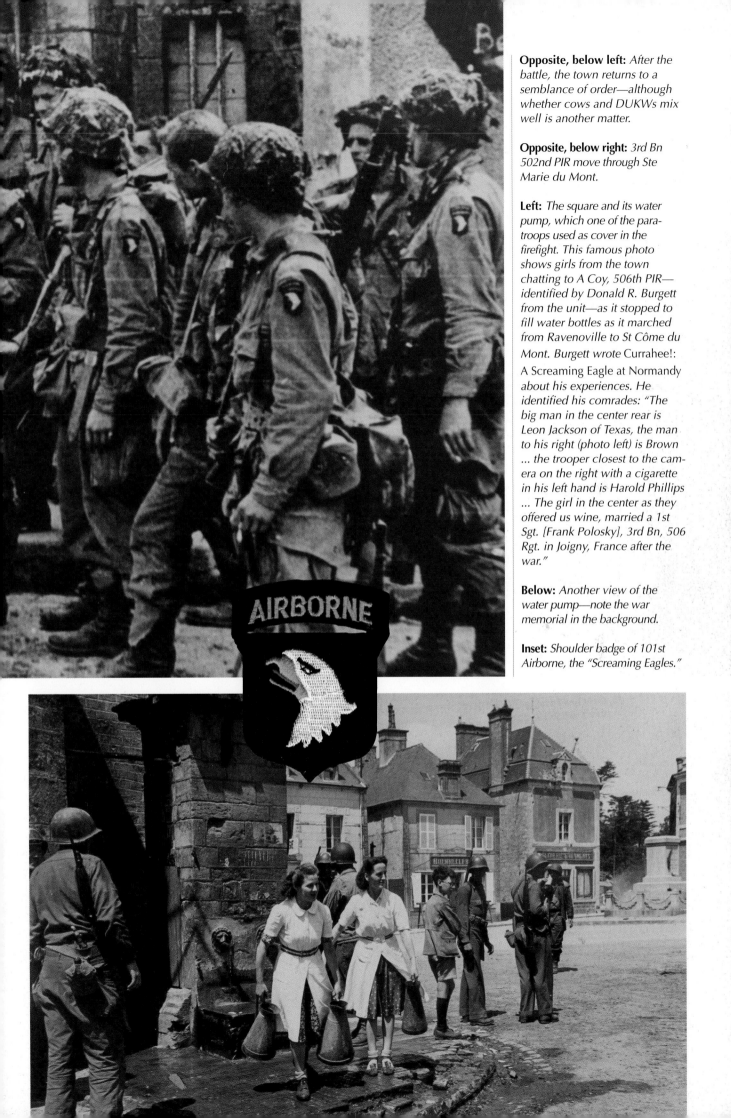

Opposite, below left: *After the battle, the town returns to a semblance of order—although whether cows and DUKWs mix well is another matter.*

Opposite, below right: *3rd Bn 502nd PIR move through Ste Marie du Mont.*

Left: *The square and its water pump, which one of the paratroops used as cover in the firefight. This famous photo shows girls from the town chatting to A Coy, 506th PIR— identified by Donald R. Burgett from the unit—as it stopped to fill water bottles as it marched from Ravenoville to St Côme du Mont. Burgett wrote* Currahee!: A Screaming Eagle at Normandy *about his experiences. He identified his comrades: "The big man in the center rear is Leon Jackson of Texas, the man to his right (photo left) is Brown ... the trooper closest to the camera on the right with a cigarette in his left hand is Harold Phillips ... The girl in the center as they offered us wine, married a 1st Sgt. [Frank Polosky], 3rd Bn, 506 Rgt. in Joigny, France after the war."*

Below: *Another view of the water pump—note the war memorial in the background.*

Inset: *Shoulder badge of 101st Airborne, the "Screaming Eagles."*

AIRBORNE

The scattered nature of the D-Day para drops is well exemplified by these photographs and the story of Capt Kenneth L. Johnson and HQ Coy of 508th PIR, 82nd Airborne. Dropped a long way from its target, photos of this unit are well known but often miscaptioned.

Left and Below: The date on these stills from a cine film is recorded as June 8. The unit is at St Marcouf, where Capt Johnson is seen talking to what are called Francs-tireurs—members of a resistance group.

Above right: Here they are seen at Ravenoville, a couple of miles southeast of St Marcouf, outside the village church (Johnson is standing with binoculars around his neck). Johnson's obituary in 1990 remembers his 33-year career through World War II, the Korean, and Vietnam wars. He received the Distinguished Service Metal, the Silver Star, the Legion of Merit with four oak leaf clusters, the Bronze Star Medal with one oak leaf cluster, the Army Commendation Medal with three oak leaf clusters, the Purple Heart, the Belgium Fourragére, the Netherland Military Order of William of Orange, the Netherland Orange Lanyard, the Combat Infantryman's Badge and the Master Parachutist Badge. He ended his career in the US Army as a major-general and is buried in Section 13 Site 6171-A of Arlington National Cemetery.

Below right: Also at Ravenoville but earlier, this June 6 photo shows men of both US airborne divisions, as photographed by Forrest Guth, outside Marmion Farm (see also page 51). The tracked vehicle is a captured Renault UE tractor and cargo trailer. The white circles on helmets distinguish the divisional artillery men.

Right: *101st Airborne was tasked with taking the lock and bridges on the Douve south of St Côme du Mont (seen here). Col Howard Johnson, CO of 501st PIR, put together a force which took the town on the 8th and went on to take the lock but the bridges were too heavily defended. On top of this—and difficult to envisage today—were the problems caused by the flooding of the low-lying ground in the area.*

Below: *Horsa gliders in background, this Willys MB jeep is towing an M3A4 Hand Cart designed to be pulled by two soldiers. Note M1 rifle in a scabbard by the windshield.*

Opposite: *Gliders coming in to LZ W at Les Forges to support 82nd Airborne.*

66

Opposite: *The battle for Carentan (seen after the battle and today) took place between June 10 and 12, when the defenders—mainly 6th Fallschirmjäger Regiment commanded by Col Friedrich von der Heydte who had retreated there from St Côme du Mont—left the town, their armor support held up by Allied air strikes and their ammunition running low. 506th PIR entered the town but a sustained counterattack by FJR6 and SS-Panzergrenadier Regiment 37 the next day pushed the airborne forces back. Forewarned of the attack by Ultra, however, Gen Bradley had sent CCA 2nd Armored to help and the Germans were halted with heavy losses.*

Above: *Troops of the 101st try out a German Kübelwagen. Its numberplate—WL 333 369—identifies that it is a Wehrmacht-Luftwaffe vehicle belonging to FJR6.*

Left: *Pvt Charles E. Rinehart (506th), Sgt James V. Longane (327th GIR), and Pvt Charles A. West (506th) pose in front of Carentan's World War I monument (see A in modern image at left).*

Below: *The intersection of the roads from St Côme du Mont, and Ste Marie du Mont is known as Dead Man's Corner. The first American tank that reached this intersection was disabled and the commander was killed. His body hung out of the tank for some time before it could be retrieved.*

British and Canadian Forces

An integral part of the Overlord plan was that on the night of June 5/6 British and American airborne forces should seize objectives at either end of the invasion beaches in order to prevent enemy counterattacks to the flanks and to facilitate the movement inland of the seaborne assault troops. On the eastern flank the British 6th Airborne, commanded by Maj-Gen Richard Gale, was given three main tasks: to capture intact the bridges over the River Orne and the Caen Canal which run close together on the eastern flank of the Sword; to capture and destroy the heavily fortified battery of 155mm guns at Merville, which enfiladed the Sword beaches and was capable severely disrupting the landings; finally, to occupy the area to the east of the landing sites and blow the bridges over the River Dives to prevent German counterattacks from that direction.

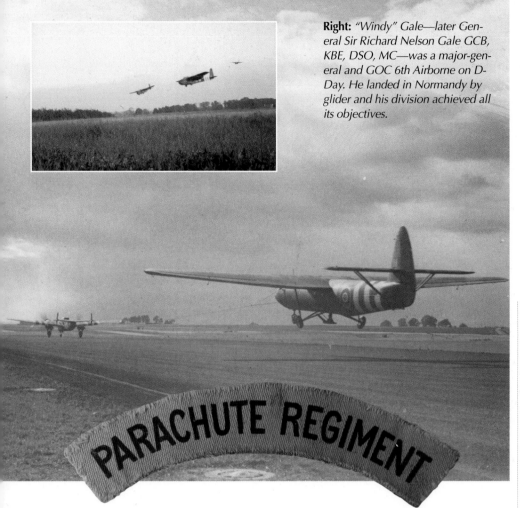

PARACHUTE REGIMENT

In essence all of these objectives would be achieved to varying degrees but not without difficulty and serious casualties in some cases. The undoubted highlight of the night was the successful capture of the Orne bridges by B and D Coys of 2nd Bn, Oxfordshire and Buckinghamshire Light Infantry, part of the 6th Airlanding Brigade. Carried in six Horsa gliders towed by Halifax bombers, they were the vanguard of the British forces that night and by a combination of accurate navigation and incredible piloting skills, three of the Horsas landed within yards of the their objective, the Caen canal bridge, which was quickly captured after a fierce firefight. At the Orne bridge the other three gliders landed further away from their objective, but in their case they found the bridge intact and undefended. To this day the first is universally known as Pegasus Bridge—the airborne badge (see page 77) shows Bellerophon riding Pegasus—and the second as Horsa Bridge in commemoration of one of the most astonishing feats of World War II.

Close behind the bridge assault came six Albermarles carrying men of the 22nd Independant Parachute Company, whose task was to land advance parties in each of three DZs (designated N, K, and V) all on the east side of the Orne. They would act as pathfinders for the main drops by setting up light signals to mark the DZs and also to activate Eureka radio beacons to guide the incoming aircraft. DZ N, closest to the bridges, was correctly marked but unfortunately one of the other Albermarles also dropped its party—intended for DZ K—onto the N area, where they also set up lights and their Eureka beacon. At Zone V, near the Merville Battery, the drop was extremely accurate, but the party's Eureka beacon was smashed on landing.

Inevitably, all this caused considerable confusion as the main wave approached. Only half of the 8th Parachute Bn landed in DZ K although the 5th Parachute Bde's drop into DZ N was much more successful and their 7th Bn was eventually able to reinforce Maj Howard's men at the bridges. The scene at DZ V was the most confused and troops landing there,

Order of Battle
6th Airborne Division
3rd Para Bde
8th (Midland Counties) Para Bn
9th (Home Counties) Para Bn
1st Canadian Para Bn
3rd Airlanding A/Tk Bty, RA
3rd Para Sqn, RE
224th Para Fd Amb, RAMC

5th Para Bde
7th (Lt Inf) Para Bn
12th (10th Bn Green Howards) Para Bn
13th (2nd/4th Bn South Lancashire Regt) Para Bn
4th Airlanding A/Tk Bty, RA
591st Para Sqn, RE
225th Para Fd Amb, RAMC

6th Airlanding Bde
1st Bn, Royal Ulster Rifles
2nd Bn, Oxfordshire & Buckinghamshire Lt Inf
12th Bn, Devonshire Regt
249th (Airborne) Fd Coy, RE
195th Airlanding Fd Amb, RAMC

Divisional Units
53rd (Worcestershire Yeomanry) Airlanding Lt Regt, RA
2 Forward (Airborne) Observation Unit, RA
2nd Airlanding LAA Bty, RA
22nd Ind Para Coy
6th Airborne Armd Recce Regt
286th (Airborne) Fd Park Coy, RE
6th AB Div Sigs
63rd, 398th, 716th Composite Coys, RASC
Glider Pilot Regt
REME, CMP, Int Corps units

Main picture: *Bénouville (A) and Ranville (B) bridges—now known as Pegasus and Horsa bridges respectively—today. The lifting bridge is a larger replacement put in place in 1994. The original is in the museum (C); Cafe Gondrée is at D. (See also photos on page 29.)*

Right: *Two of the Horsa gliders that brought Maj John Howard and men of D Coy, 2nd Bn, Oxfordshire and Buckinghamshire Light Infantry. The building visible across the canal is Cafe Gondrée.*

Below right: *Cafe Gondrée today—the Pegasus Bridge Cafe.*

Top: *Bénouville Bridge and the Canal de Caen. Cafe Gondrée is the building nearest the bridge on the opposite bank at A and is said to be the first French house to be liberated on D-Day.*

Above: *Two of the Horsa gliders (see page 71) are visible on the far bank of the canal at B.*

Right and Opposite: *The view today. The bust of John Howard (right) is at C, and sits near the spot that his Horsa glider came to rest on June 6—the three identified by cairns (D). Howard led Operation Deadstick—the coup de main on this and Ranville Bridge that spanned the adjacent River Orne. The British took the bridges within ten minutes of arrival, having taken the enemy by complete surprise, at a cost of but two casualties. They held the bridges until relieved, first by Lord Lovat's 1st SpS Bde, to the accompaniment of piper Bill Millin, and later by 2nd Bn, Royal Warwickshire Regt. At E is a RM Centaur tank.*

72

Inset, above: *Cap badge of The Parachute Regiment.*

Above: *The rear of Merville Battery's type H611 concrete Casemate 1 at right; Casemates 2 and 3 are visible at left.*

Opposite, above left and right: *Plan of the battery and aerial recce photo of the area after bombing. The battery was taken by assault by around 150 men of the 9th Parachute Bn—rather fewer than the 750 sent to do the job. The survivors—some 75–80 men—then moved on to attack La Plein.*

Opposite, below *The battery museum today includes a C-47 Dakota of US Ninth Air Force that had taken part in the Normandy landings. It was acquired by the museum in 2007 from Sarajevo.*

including the 1st Canadian Parachute Bn, were widely scattered, many dropping into the flooded fields bordering the River Dives where many drowned, weighed down by parachutes and heavy equipment.

The 9th Parachute Bn under Col TerenceOtway was tasked with the capture of the Merville Battery which was to be softened up by a force of 100 Lancaster bombers. These arrived on time but most of bombs went wide of the target. Eleven Horsa gliders were then due to bring in explosives and other equipment for the destruction of the battery but only four managed to land within a mile of the objective, still too far away. Otway's own men were scattered and he could only muster around 160 men out of what should have been some 750. Nevertheless, he pressed ahead with the attack and despite the half of his force becoming casualties the battery was taken,. Disappointingly, it was discovered that only light 75mm guns were mounted, the heavier pieces having been temporarily removed. Doing what damage he could (his demolitions team and explosives had not reached the battery) Otway was forced to leave to continue its mission. The battery's commander, Oberleutnant Raimund Steiner, returned and was able to recommission two of the guns and defend the battery against an attack by No 3 Commando on June 7.

Scattered groups of the 8th Parachute and 1st Canadian Bns managed to secure and destroy the bridges over the River Dives, thus securing the division's eastern flank. Throughout the night Horsa gliders continued to arrive bringing in heavy equipment such as jeeps, radios and anti-tank guns.

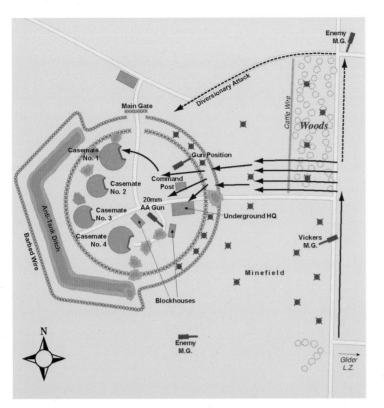

Maj-Gen Gale, the divisional commander, landed in a lift of 48 gliders which successfully landed on DZ N, and set up headquarters at the Chateau de Haume near Ranville. At around the same time three Hamilcar gliders, larger than a Horsa, arrived carrying precious 17pdr anti-tank guns—the best Allied anti-tank weapon of the war.

By the morning of the 6th, all of the main objectives had been achieved but during the day the airborne forces came under attack from the south-east by units of 21st Panzer Division, one of the first to react to the allied landings. There was some desperate fighting but the paratroopers held out, supported by gunfire from the cruiser HMS *Mauritius* offshore. In the evening the 6th Airlanding Bde arrived in no fewer than 258 gliders, including 30 of the large Hamilcars. In addition troops from the 3rd Division which had landed on Sword together with the Commandos of the 1st Special Service Bde had also joined up with the airborne forces. In the week after D-Day these forces came under increasing pressure from the 21st Panzer and 346th Infantry Divisions until a fierce battle on the night of June 12, in which Bréville was occupied by the 12th Parachute Bn, finally secured the Allied position. 6th Airborne had done its job but at some cost. Even today it is impossible to establish the exact number of casualties but it is estimated that around 1,500 men were killed or missing in action on D-Day itself and many more in the following days. For example, the 12th Battalion lost over 100 men in the attack on Bréville. Nevertheless, the division could be proud of its achievements and had made a vital contribution to the success of Overlord.

Above: *The Airborne badge depicts Bellerophon riding Pegasus. It was designed by Edward Seago, from a suggestion by the famous novelist Daphne du Maurier, the wife of Maj-Gen "Boy" Browning, commander of 1st Airborne. It was worn by all British Airborne troops.*

Opposite, above: *LZ N was west of Ranville Bridge and south-west of the village of Am-fréville.*

Opposite, inset: *The 12th (York-shire) Parachute Bn was supposed to have dropped on DZ N, but the drop was scattered. Nevertheless, the unit helped capture Ranville and held it against repeated German counterattacks. Later, 12th Bn, in conjunction with D Coy of the 12th Devons took Bréville in a bloody battle during which they lost 9 officers and 153 men. Here, men of the 12th Parachute Bn's MG Pl give the thumbs up for the camera on June 10, having just joined their unit after the drop. L–R: Dave Weightman, Phil Gudgeon, Jack Thorpe, Bill Armstrong, Willy Watkins, Fred Browning, Tom Matthews, Unknown, and Spike Walker (kneeling).*

Opposite, below: *A Sherman of 13th/18th Royal Hussars in action against German troops using crashed Horsa gliders as cover near Ranville, June 10.*

Left: *Map showing the drop zones and area of operations of 6th Airborne.*

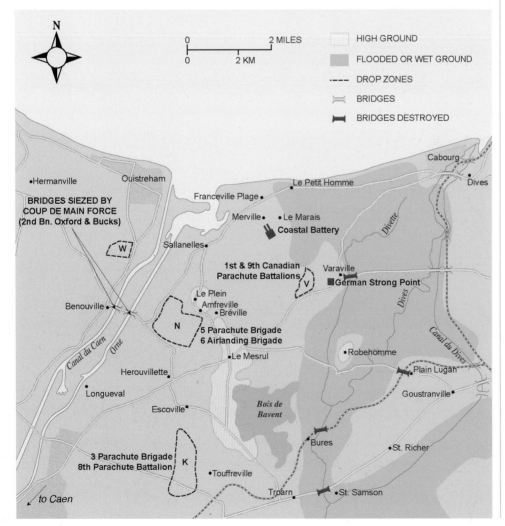

Right: *Gen Sir Bernard Montgomery, commander of the 21st Army Group, decorating L/Cpl Russell Geddes of the 1st Canadian Parachute Bn with the Military Medal during an investiture in Normandy, July 16. The Canadians had joined 3rd Parachute Bde in 1943 in what Lt-Gen Sir Napier Crookenden later described as "a happy association from the beginning." They arrived in France in 50 aircraft to secure the DZ and destroy road bridges over the Dives. Landing between 01:00 and 01:30 on June 6, they accomplished all their tasks: the bridges on the Dives and Divette in Varaville and Robehomme were cut; the left flank of the 9th Parachute Bn at Merville was secured; and the crossroads at Le Mesnil was taken. They would return home at the end of the war with a VC (won on the Rhine by Cpl Topham), an OBE, three MCs, an MBE, a DCM, and nine MMs.*

Opposite, clockwise from bottom left: *Practice drop of the battalion over Salisbury Plain, February 1944. Crookenden talks of the Canadians' first learning experience when they joined the British: getting used to dropping without the reserve chute the Canadians, following American doctrine, were used to.*

The battalion in a transit camp staging area prior to D-Day, early June 1944.

The shoulder and cap badges of the battalion.

The cost of war: Brothers Lts Joseph Maurice Rousseau (left) and Joseph Philippe Rousseau at a transit camp near Down Ampney, England, February 13, 1944. Both officers were later killed in action, Philippe on June 7 and Maurice on September 20, 1944.

1 CANADIAN PARACHUTE BATTALION

CANADIAN PARACHUTE CORPS

CHAPTER 5
UTAH BEACH

Gooseberry No. 1 breakwater off Utah Beach showing the gap caused as German shelling interrupted the positioning of George S. Wasson.

"We'll start the war from right here!"
Gen. Theodore Roosevelt Jr after discovering the Utah landings were a mile off course

Order of Battle
US VII Corps
4th Inf Div
8th, 12th, 22nd Inf Regts
HHB, 1st Div Arty
20th, 29th, 42nd, 44th Fd
  Arty Bns
4th Sigs Coy
704th Ord Lt Maint Coy
4th QM Coy
4th Recon Tp
4th Engr Bn
4th Med Bn

90th Inf Div
357th, 358th, 359th Inf
  Regt
HHB, 90th Div Arty
343rd, 344th, 345th, 915th
  Fd Arty Bns
90th Sigs Coy
790th Ord Lt Maint Coy
90th QM Coy
90th Recon Tp
315th Engr Bn
315th Med Bn

4th Cav Gp (Mechanized)
4th Cav Sqn
24th Cav Sqn

6th Armd Gp
70th Tank Bn
746th Tank Bn

Various non-Divisional
  troops

Below: *Convoy of LSTs heading for the beaches, June 6. Note each has its own barrage balloon.*

Opposite: *Aerial photograph and (below) map of Utah Beach, showing actual (A–B) and intended landing areas (C–D) as carried up the beach by Lt–Col Paul W. Steinbeck.*

Taken from the citation for his Congressional Medal of Honor: "For gallantry and intrepidity at the risk of his life above and beyond the call of duty ... Brig-Gen Roosevelt ... repeatedly led groups from the beach, over the seawall and established them inland. His valor, courage, and presence in the very front of the attack and his complete unconcern at being under heavy fire inspired the troops to heights of enthusiasm and self-sacrifice."

The landings on Utah are remembered today as being the easiest of the five D-Day sectors: by the end of June 6, over 23,000 men and 1,500 vehicles had been landed for a loss of fewer than 200.

It could all have been very different, but for two factors. The first was the tide which pushed the invasion fleet south by over a mile—something that the fog of war didn't make clear until the first troops landed. The second was the presence with the first wave of the forces assaulting the enemy-held beaches of Brig-Gen Ted Roosevelt III—son of President Teddy Roosevelt. Aged 56, second-in-command of the lead unit, 4th Infantry Division, he was the oldest man in the invasion and the only general to land with the first wave of troops. Gen Roosevelt realized what had happened, conducted his own recon, and identified that it wasn't a problem. "We'll start the war from here," was his famous summation of the position.

Fate had provided the right leader for the moment, as was recognized by his Medal of Honor. It had also kept the 4th Division away from the strongpoint at Varreville and further away from the batteries of Crisbecq and Azeville. Without the high ground that gave the defenders at Omaha so much strength, distracted by the paratroop and glider drops inland, the defenders of Utah were mopped up relatively easily. Indeed, the inundated low-lying coastal areas proved more of a hindrance than the Atlantic Wall.

Roosevelt's citation for the medal of Honor ends, "Under his seasoned, precise, calm, and unfaltering leadership, assault troops reduced beach strong points and rapidly moved inland with minimum casualties. He thus contributed substantially to the successful establishment of the beachhead in France."

It was a pothsumous decoration: Ted Roosevelt died on July 12, just after Gen. Omar Bradley had put him forward for promotion to major-general and the command of 90th Division. Eisenhower called to approve the plan but heard that Roosevelt had died of a heart attack during the night.

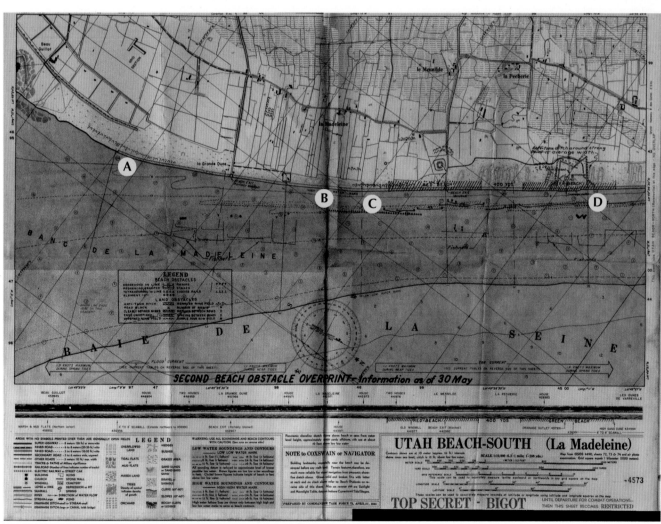

Top: USS Nevada *provided support for the troops on the Cotentin peninsula June 6–17. She was straddled by shore batteries but not hit.*

Above: *Assault elements of Force U, including DD tanks, were still on the beaches when this photo was taken shortly after H-Hour. The amphibious tanks await the blowing of breaches in the sea wall.*

Above right: *Plan of WN 5, the strongpoint that defended what became the main exit from the beach. Today's museum sits on the site of a Tobruk that boasted a 37mm Renault tank turret, which has been incorporated into the museum. Further down the beach (see pages 90–93) there is a monument to the engineers who cleared the beach of obstacles on D-Day. It is mounted on top of a Type 702 bunker, one of five in this area. The largest guns were 50mm and 47mm, the former housed in Type 667 casemates. The area behind the coastline was flooded to the west and surrounded by barbed wire and minefields, forcing the attackers to use the narrow roads that led off the beach inland.*

Right: *A French 1937 47mm A/Tk weapon at WN 5—not strong enough to withstand the initial bombardment. At sea can be seen a Rhino ferry. Two bulldozers work on the beach.*

Opposite: *Congestion at the beachhead as more troops land.*

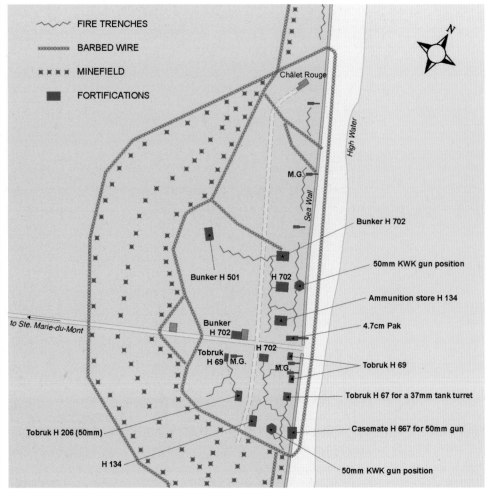

FIRE TRENCHES

BARBED WIRE

MINEFIELD

FORTIFICATIONS

Châlet Rouge

High Water

M.G.

Sea Wall

Bunker H 702

Bunker H 501

50mm KWK gun position

H 702

Ammunition store H 134

to Ste. Marie-du-Mont

Bunker H 702

4.7cm Pak

Tobruk H 69 M.G.

H 702

M.G.

Tobruk H 69

Tobruk H 67 for a 37mm tank turret

Tobruk H 206 (50mm)

Casemate H 667 for 50mm gun

H 134

50mm KWK gun position

Above: *Color images of the Normandy landings are rare—particularly since an aircrash killed one of the Signal Corps team, Steve Stevens, who took them, and most of the footage was lost. This photo is probably of Utah as the man on the right wears the shoulder insignia of 1st Engineer Special Bde (ESB) and the one behind has the ESB blue ring on his helmet. 1st ESB carried out such essential tasks as laying roadway over and clearing obstructions.*

Right and Inset, above: *Follow-up troops make their way to the beach.*

Inset, center: *USS* Bayfield *was the name ship of a class of attack transports. Launched in 1943, she brought troops across the Atlantic in 1944 and became HQ and flagship for Rear Adm Don Pardee Moon, Commander, Force U due to land at Utah Beach.* Bayfield *took 8th Inf Regt (4th Division) to Utah, and after the troops had disembarked provided hospital facilities as well as acting as flagship, leaving the Normandy coast on June 25.*

Inset, below: *Combat medics of the 4th Division help wounded men from the 2nd Naval Beach Bn near Exit 2, on June 6 or 7.*

Above: *A Dodge truck, its .50 Browning MG gunner looking out for aircraft, disembarks from an LCT in front of the Chalet Rouge landmark to the north of WN 5 on Uncle Red Beach.*

Right: *The 237th Engr Combat Bn landed with the infantry, and under fire, waded ashore with 60lb packs of explosives, cleared the beaches of mines, and blew gaps in the seawall in advance of the rising tide. For their service the unit received a Presidential Unit Citation and the provisional French Government awarded it the French Croix de Guerre with Silver Star. Once the beach had been cleared, bulldozers opened up the roadways and the advance began.*

Below right: *US Navy personnel—probably from 2nd Naval Beach Bn—examine remote-controlled Goliath tracked demolition charges found unused on the beach.*

Opposite, above and center: *Follow-up troops in cover behind the seawall. Shelling of the beach continued for some time as this explosion on June 11 shows.*

Above: *Danish sailors monument at Ste Marie du Mont. This monument is dedicated to the 800 Danish sailors who were involved in the D-Day landings*

Left: *Follow-up troops prepare to land at Utah.*

Top: *American troops land on Utah Beach. Brig-Gen Theodore Roosevelt, Jr, at age 56, was the oldest soldier—and the only general—to land with the assault troops on D-Day. It was as well he did. He was able to coordinate the attack after the landing craft reached land half a mile off course. A identifies Exit 2 from which the troops left Uncle Red Beach.*

Right and Above: *Located on the beach of La Madeleine, the Utah Beach Museum was built around the strategic bunker WN 5, in the exact place where American troops arrived on French soil. Extensively renovated in 2011, it now includes a replica B-26 visible through the roof in the above photo.*

Right: *German PoWs sit under the watchful eyes of men from 1st ESB awaiting transfer to England. The Georgien cloth badge at A (and inset) shows that this soldier is from Georgia— either a volunteer or one of the many foreigners conscripted into the German Army. Ost Bataillon 795 (Georgien) fought the 505th PIR at Ste Mère Église and surrendered on D+1.*

Below: *There are a number of memorials at Utah Beach: the main picture looks from the new US Navy Memorial, a 12-foot high bronze memorial, toward the memorial to the 1st ESB. The inset image shows the complex: at B, the World War II Utah Beach American Memorial which commemorates the achievements of American troops of the VII Corps who landed and fought in the liberation of the Cotentin Peninsula from June 6 to July 1, 1944. At C is the memorial to the 90th Inf Div. At D the memorial to 1st ESB, and at E the US Navy Memorial.*

Above and Below: The flow of men and materiel through Utah Beach wasn't as fast as had been hoped: 20–24,000 men landed on D-Day along with 1,700 vehicles; on D+1 another 10,000 men and 1,500 vehicles. However, as can be seen from these photos, the gradual slope of the beach meant that landing craft couldn't get closer to the exits and more DUKWs had to be requisitioned.

Left: D+1 saw the final two glider drops of Operation Neptune—codenamed Galverston and Hackensack. Some 200 gliders delivered 2,258 men, 20 artillery pieces, and 75 vehicles to reinforce 82nd Airborne.

Above: *Much of the area behind the beach had been flooded (see map opposite) which hindered progress. It also meant that troops kept the waterproofing on their equipment where possible. The first man in line still has the Pliofilm cover to his rifle and has rigged a makeshift sling for it. Under his right arm he carries a 2.36in bazooka to which is attached an inflated lifebelt. Note the assault gasmask bags they all have on their chests.*

Left: *With his M1926 lifebelt still around his waist, this member of a machine-gun team carries an M1917 Browning and belts of .30 ammunition. The gunner carried the tripod, his assistant the gun; usually there were two other members of the team, an assistant to carry water/ammo/tools and an ammo carrier who also had a rifle to protect the team during setup. The wartime caption identifies his unit as 1/8th Inf Regt, part of 4th Inf Div.*

Opposite, above: *4th Infantry Division—the "Ivy" Division, a play on words based on the roman numeral IV; see inset unit badge—spearheaded the invasion on Utah Beaches, and after taking the strongpoints headed inland from the beaches to make contact with the paratroops as shown in the above map.*

Opposite, below: *This unit carries a variety of equipment. At extreme left, the tripod for the .30 Browning MG carried by the man at extreme right (note the coiled water-pipe around the barrel). Next to the tripod carrier is a signaler carrying wire; further back there's a medic carrying a stretcher.*

Map Legend

← AXIS OF ADVANCE

━━ NIGHT POSITIONS, 6 JUNE

GLIDER LANDING ZONE W

GERMAN STRONG POINT

GERMAN POCKET BETWEEN 8TH INF. AND 505th PRCHT INF.

Ravenoville

Homel de Gruffes
3/22

les Dunes de Varreville

Foucarville

3/22

St. Germain-de- Varreville
1/22

Beuzeville-au-Plain

Exit 4   1/22, 2/22

3/22

1/12   2/22

Bandienville

St. Martin-de-Varreville

Neuville-au-Plain

2/12   3/12

359(-)
44

1/8

la Madeleine

TD 899

Exit 3   12th Inf.

la Grand Dune

505(-) Prcht

Ste. Mère-Eglise

A 70

746

la Fière

1/8   42

Audoville la-Hubert

Beaches as established

Merderet

Turqueville

Beau Guillot

Ecoqueneauville

Culvert out
65

Fouville

3/8

la Houssaye

Exit 2

Chef-du-Pont

K 8   K/8(-)

3/8(-)

Germain

Exit 1   2/8

les Forges

Pouppeville

70(L)
2/8

29

Lock Position

Garqueput

Ste. Marie-du-Mont

le Port

G/8

Hiesville

le Grand Vey

Beuzeville-la-Bastille

Vierville

0   1 MILE
0   1 KM

190467

The Utah area was more difficult to defend than Omaha—there was little high ground and for this reason, the German defenders flooded large areas behind the coast, which did much to hinder American progress. There were a number of Widerstandsnester and Stützpunkten as shown here.

Right: WN 10 is sited on the original Tare Green Beach where the landings should have taken place. A Type H612 casemate housed a 75mm; an 88mm PaK 43/41 gave cover over the northern sector of the beach. Two other casemates housed a command post and Skoda 47mm guns. It was covered by SP 9 from the south, and was also supported by an M19 mortar, several Renault tank turrets mounted on Tobruks, many machine guns, minefields, and A/Tk ditches.

Above: *WN 8 lies on the coast at Audouville la Hubert. Its main armament was a 75mm field gun, supplemented by 47mm cannon, two 50mm AA guns, and Tobruks housing six MG positions and a mortar. The troops stationed here were billeted in Type 622 (seen here) and 502 bunkers. The site was surrounded by minefields and anti-tank ditches.*

Above and Below left: *Just to the north of WN 8, south of the dunes of Varreville, is SP 9. It housed two 88mm guns in Type 667 casemates facing north and south, had a bunker for a 150cm searchlight, and a Type 633 mortar bunker (below). It was taken by 3rd Bn, 22nd Inf Regt.*

Right: *Aerial view of the Crisbecq or Saint Marcouf Battery, showing one of the casemates (No 1) housing a Skoda 210mm gun. Although never completed, the battery's three, long-range guns threatened Utah Beach and the naval task force, which was proved when the battery engaged and sank the destroyer USS* Corry *on D-Day. Subsequently silenced by fire from battleships USS* Arkansas, *USS* Nevada, *and USS* Texas, *the battery repaired one of its guns and continued shelling and withstood sustained attacks from the sea and land forces, at one stage calling on the Azeville battery to fire on their own position to disperse their attackers—elements of 4th Division. Crisbecq was finally taken at 08:20 on June 12, after the German commandant (Oberleutnant Walter Ohmsen) ordered the 67 (of some 400) Kriegsmarine (German Navy) troops able to do so to evacuate to a new defensive line toward Cherbourg. This left the battery defenseless and it was taken on the 12th by 39th Inf Regt of 9th Inf Div.*

Inset, left: *Plan of the site.*

Inset, right: *The fire-control bunker.*

Below: *One of the Czech-built Skoda K52 210mm guns in its Type 683 casemate (No 2) which allowed a 120-degree arc of fire.*

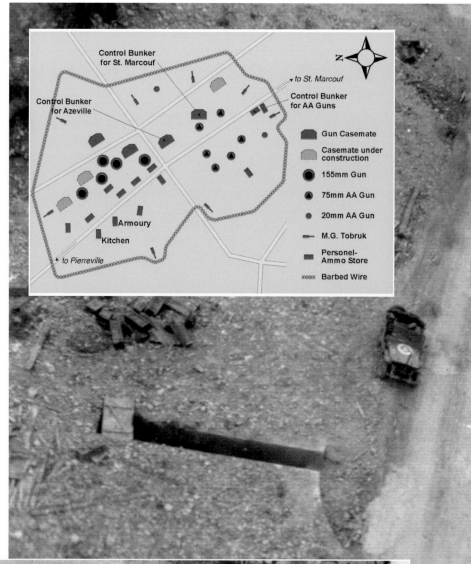

191499

*The "Big Red One"
memorial above Omaha Beach.
In the distance at right
Arromanches and the remains of
the Mulberry Harbor—see also
page 121.*

CHAPTER 6
OMAHA BEACH

"Two kinds of men are staying on this beach,
the dead and those who are going to die.
Now let's get the hell out of here."

Col George Taylor, CO of 16th Infantry Regiment, 1st Infantry Divison

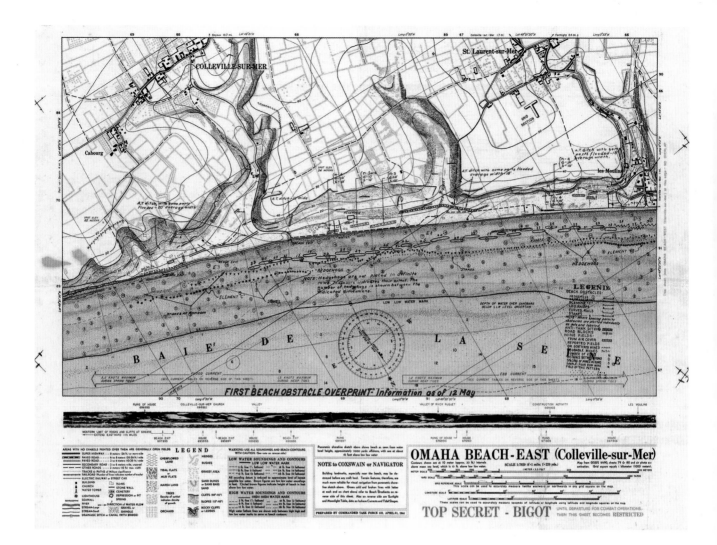

The map labels include: COLLEVILLE-SUR-MER, St. Laurent-sur-Mer, Cabourg, les Moulins, BAIE DE LA SEINE.

FIRST BEACH OBSTACLE OVERPRINT: Information as of 12 May

LEGEND

NOTE to COXSWAIN or NAVIGATOR

OMAHA BEACH-EAST (Colleville-sur-Mer)

TOP SECRET - BIGOT

Above and Above right:
Detailed maps of the Omaha beaches. The "BIGOT" reference appeared on all paper elements of the invasion plan. A security classification beyond Top Secret, the codeword was apparently chosen by reversing "To Gib," words stamped on the papers of officers going to Gibraltar for Operation Torch. The maps provided the most recent information on the defenses from aerial photos, French resistance fighters, Allied frogmen who examined the geology of the beaches as well as their physical characteristics. All along the bottom of each map is a watercolor. National Geographic *talked to a number of the artists of these, including Navy Lt William A. Bostick who was especially proud of an overlay and chart that allowed navigators to see when their type of craft would beach.*

Opposite: *A classic view of Omaha.* After the Battle *times this at 07:40–08:00.*

Of the five beaches attacked on June 6, Omaha saw the sternest fighting. As has been so graphically portrayed in *Saving Private Ryan*, well-placed defenders on the high ground and extensive beach defenses did their job. On top of this, so much had gone wrong with the first wave: many of the amphibious DD Sherman tanks didn't reach the beach. They were released from their landing craft too far away where the greater swell swamped them and the troops landing on Omaha missed their firepower. Another problem was that many units landed in the wrong place. Strong tides and winds carried the landing craft off line and led to confusion. Finally, the German emplacements and defenses were well-placed on high ground and the only cover on the beach—the seawall—was over a killing ground. There were 32 fortified areas located between the Vire River and Port-en-Bessin: in all, 12 of these strongpoints were able to direct fire on Omaha Beach.

The attacking forces—units of the US 29th and 1st Inf Divs—suffered over 2,000 casualties (initially reported as 1,190 1st Div, 743 29th Div, 441 corps troops with 694 killed), many of them drowned during the approach, but led by US Rangers, themselves misplaced (they were the follow-up troops to Rudder's Rangers who had scaled the Pointe du Hoc) the American troops pushed forward and by nightfall, they had gained hold of the beach and its immediate hinterland. Despite the casualties, 34,000 troops had been landed by the end of the day.

Today, on the high ground above the beach, sits the American cemetery at Colleville, laid out in an area of 170 acres which was ceded to the United States by the French government. A new visitor center explains the history. Outside, the cemetery contains 9,387 gravestones. Every day at 16:30, visitors can watch the ceremony of the Lowering of the Colors. To the sound of a military hymn, the American flag is lowered and folded.

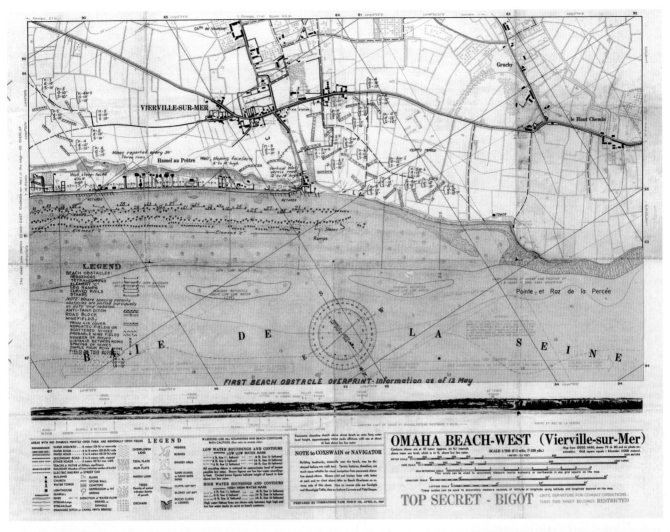

At the western end of Omaha Beach, the Pointe du Hoc Battery was a potent threat. It was attacked early on June 6 by the US Ranger Assault Group under the command of Lt-Col James E. Rudder. The plan (right) called for the cliffs to be scaled. In spite of the pre-attack bombardment (far right), the unit sustained significant casualties in its daring attack, but took the position and held it until relieved on D+2 in spite of counterattacks from the German 916th Grenadier Regt. The guns, however, were not there. The Germans had moved them inland. Rudder sent out a patrol that found five of the six guns nearby and destroyed them.

Left and Below: *Today, the photos of Pointe du Hoc show much traveled paths. The granite pylon (left and A below) is the Ranger Monument.*

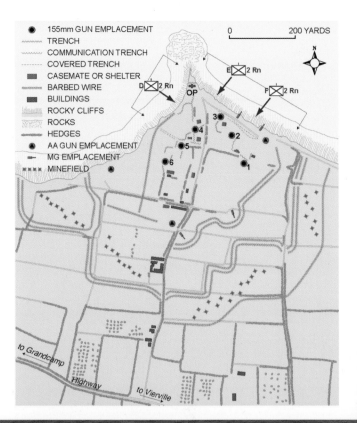

155mm GUN EMPLACEMENT
TRENCH
COMMUNICATION TRENCH
COVERED TRENCH
CASEMATE OR SHELTER
BARBED WIRE
BUILDINGS
ROCKY CLIFFS
ROCKS
HEDGES
AA GUN EMPLACEMENT
MG EMPLACEMENT
MINEFIELD

0   200 YARDS

N

E 2 Rn

D 2 Rn   F 2 Rn

OP

3
4
2
5
1
6

to Grandcamp

Highway   to Vierville

Above, Opposite, above, and Bottom right: *Taken in 1943 (***above***) before the bombardment, this photograph shows well the 100ft cliffs that the Germans thought were impregnable. In fact, the naval bombardment caused a cliff fall (visible in photo* **bottom right***) that left a 40ft pile of rubble and considerably reduced the climbing required.*

Right: *The prominent Stars and Stripes flag is to stop friendly fire problems—some Rangers were lost to Allied tank fire by the relieving force on D+2.*

Below right: *The assault. Nine LCAs reached the beach with Coys D, E, and F of 2nd Ranger Bn on board. The follow-up troops, however, missed the message that the pointe had been taken and so continued on to Omaha with 116th RCT. In fact, landing at 07:10, within five minutes the Rangers were at the top of the cliffs—thanks to covering fire by the destroyer Satterlee. When they reached the top the Rangers discovered that the guns were absent. Immediately, patrols went out to find them while the main body consolidated its position, but it would not be until later in the day that the final German resistance was quashed. In the meantime the patrols discovered the guns about 800 yards away, ready to fire on the beaches. They destroyed them with thermite grenades. The Rangers then had to hold against German counterattacks, and did so heroically until relief—in the form of 5th Rangers, 116th Inf Regt, and 743nd Tk Bn—arrived on the 8th. Initially, the Rangers were fired on by the relieving forces and lost some troops to friendly fire.*

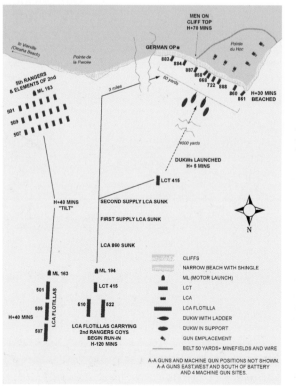

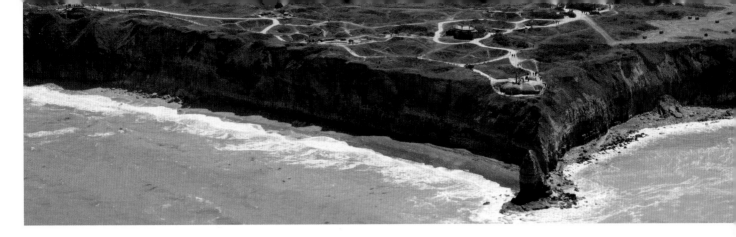

Far left and Left: *The cliffs west of Vierville form the Point et Raz de la Perce on which was sited a radar station (left). It was attacked by 2nd Rangers, but they arrived to find that HMS Glasgow had already destroyed it from the sea. The cliffs allowed an enfilade of the sweep of Omaha and a number of guns, including this 50mm (far left) were sited above Vierville.*

Below: *The 116th RCT zone, which was to have the firepower of 64 tanks, half from the 741st Tk Bn and half from the 743rd. Those from the 741st launched into a heavy swell, foundered, and only two of 27 reached the beach; the other three were landed by the LCT. After the Battle quotes French diver Jacques Lemonchois as having found two of the tanks beneath the waves, some nine miles offshore. Without the tanks to destroy the strongpoints, the infantry arrived like ducks in a shooting gallery.*

D-1
VIERVILLE

D-3
LES MOULINS

WESTERN BEACHES, 116TH RCT

EASTERN

D-1
VIERVILLE

D-3
LES MOULINS

E-1

E-

ST LAURENT-SUR-MER

Order of Battle

US V Corps

16th RCT of 1st Inf Div
16th Inf Regt
741st Tk Bn
Special Engr Task Force
7th Fd Arty Bn
62nd Armd Fd Arty Bn
197th AAA Bn
1st Engr Bn
5th ESB
20th Engr Combat Bn
81st CW Bn

116th RCT of 29th Inf Div
116th Inf Regt
C Coy, 2nd Ranger Bn
5th Ranger Bn
743rd Tk Bn
Special Engr Task Force
111th Fd Arty Bn
58th Armd Fd Arty Bn
4677th AAA Bn
121st Engr Bn
6th ESB
112th Engr Combat Bn
81st CW Bn
461st Amphibious Truck
    Coy

18th RCT of 1st Inf Div
18th Inf Regt
745th Tk Bn
32nd and 5th Fd Arty Bn
5th ESB

115th RCT of 29th Inf Div
115th Inf Regt
110th Fd Arty Bn

26th RCT of 1st Inf Div
26th Inf Regt
33rd Fd Arty Bn

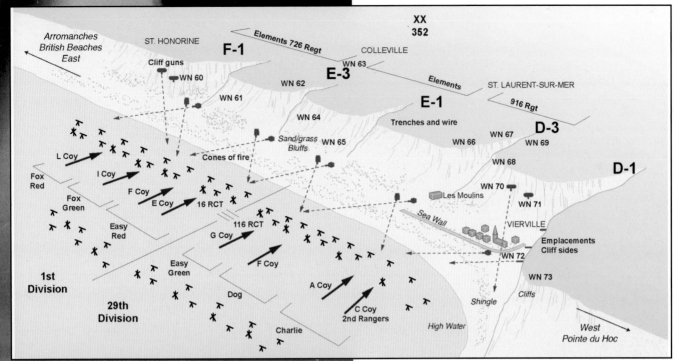

Map labels:
- Arromanches / British Beaches / East
- ST. HONORINE
- Cliff guns
- WN 60
- WN 61
- F-1
- Elements 726 Regt
- XX / 352
- COLLEVILLE
- WN 63
- E-3
- WN 62
- Elements
- ST. LAURENT-SUR-MER
- E-1
- WN 64
- Trenches and wire
- 916 Rgt
- D-3
- WN 65
- Sand/grass Bluffs
- WN 67
- WN 69
- WN 66
- WN 68
- D-1
- Cones of fire
- L Coy
- I Coy
- Fox Red
- F Coy
- Fox Green
- E Coy
- 16 RCT
- Easy Red
- 116 RCT
- G Coy
- Les Moulins
- WN 70
- WN 71
- Sea Wall
- VIERVILLE
- Easy Green
- F Coy
- Emplacements Cliff sides
- WN 72
- 1st Division
- 29th Division
- Dog
- A Coy
- C Coy 2nd Rangers
- WN 73
- Charlie
- Shingle
- Cliffs
- High Water
- West / Pointe du Hoc

IES, 16TH RCT

F-1

COLLEVILLE

Left and Above: *The five "draws"—from the west, D-1, D-3, E-1, E-3, and F-1—were the exits to the beach, cutting through the bluffs that dominate the seafront between the cliffs west of Vierville and to the east at St Honorine-les-Perts. The defenders had the high ground, the Widerstandsnester—hardened MG shelters—and bunkers with heavier weapons, and beach defenses. The attackers had naval guns, numbers, and the will to win. Initially, the two RCTs, 16th (1st Div) to the east and 116th (29th Div) to the west, foundered on the foreshore, but pushed on by the second wave, by C Coy, 2nd Rangers at Vierville, and with great bravery, the US forces carried the day. By nightfall, they had pushed far enough inland to gain a foothold on the Continent.*

Top left: *The most basic sea defense was the Hemmelbalk—a heavy wooden construction, positioned with the long sloping side toward the sea, below the high tide line. As the landing craft approached the beach they would ride up the sloped side and as they tried to withdraw the top end would puncture the hull of the vessel. To increase the damage inflicted, steel teeth were sometimes attached to the top, and these obstacles, like all types, were often mined.*

Above left: *Heavy wooden posts, often topped with Tellermines or any other explosive device that could be adapted to suit, were also used. The rate at which these could be installed in sandy beaches was greatly increased when it was found that a suitable hole could be dug in a matter of seconds using high pressure hoses. On shingle or rocky areas progress was much slower as the pit had to be dug by hand and the post often had to be concreted in.*

Right and Inset: *Vierville, at the western end of Omaha, was the location of Charlie and Dog Green beaches and the most heavily defended area. Carefully Widerstandsnester: 70–73 with 4 A/Tk casemates, 10 MG bunkers or Tobruks, and four mortar Tobruks—created an awful killing zone that decimated the first wave of the 116th RCT. With the attack stalled and further landings temporarily suspended, action by shallower drafted destroyers and the inspirational leadership of the 5th Rangers, got things moving. Various significant memorials and locations are identified:*

A *The National Guard monument sits atop the Type 677 88mm casemate. In 1944 an anti-tank wall ran across the road from this bunker. It was breached by the actions of the 29th Div combat engineers—a plaque remembers the 121st ECB although some identify the 147th ESB as the unit involved.*

B *A stele dedicated to 29th Div that made up the 116th RCT which attacked the west side of Omaha. 29th Div unit badge inset opposite.*

C *The stele celebrating the soldiers of 6th Special Engineer Bde.*

D *By the side of the road there's a length of bridge that was part of the St Laurent-sur-Mer Mulberry Harbor, which was erected by June 16, but was destroyed by the storm of June 19*

E *WN 71 was on the bluff above the D517. An observation point for WN 72, it was well defended with Tobruks for MGs and mortars.*

F and Opposite, below *WN 72's Type 667 bunker housed an 88mm Pak 43 which proved extremely successful in the defense.*

G and Right *Another of WN 72's casemates, this one held a 50mm gun that proved effective against landing craft and tanks. The two WN 72 bunkers, and WN 73 on the cliffs to the west, enfiladed the beach.*

110

Main photo: *Fires caused by naval gunfire provided some obscuration of Dog Red and Dog White beaches opposite the D-3 Les Moulins draw. This helped reduce the casualties to the east of the draw where Coy F, 116th RCT landed.*

Inset photos, this page:
Above: *The D-3 draw today is the site of two important monuments:*
A *The Liberation, 1st Division, and 116th RCT monument has inscriptions on the sides dedicated to the Big Red One and to the 116th RCT of the 29th Div.*
B *"Les Braves" by artist Anilore Banon is a more recent scuulpture (dating from 2004) in memory of the bravery of those who fought on the beach.*

Below: *There was a great deal of damage to the civilian structures around Omaha and many civilian deaths. The population of Normandy welcomed their liberators, but the Allied armies paid scant attention to the needs of those they liberated.*

Inset photos, opposite:
Left: *A detailed diagram of the defenses of Draw D-3, which was protected by two Widerstandsnester, one of which (WN 68) was still under construction. Further up the valley was WN 67, with a Nebelwerfer rocket launcher.*

Above right: *Close-up of a Ranger in an LCA at Weymouth. He's carrying a bazooka and, in his right hand, the grey cardboard box which contained his life preserver. The tube of a Bangalore torpedo sticks up to the left. The 5th Rangers landed on Dog White Beach where the Gap Assault Team intended for Dog Green had managed to blow a gap in the beach defenses. Exhorted by 29th Div Gen "Dutch" Cota to "lead the way," the Rangers did just that and headed up the bluff.*

Below right: *There was little that Gen Omar Bradley (second from left) could do on USS Augusta but watch and worry. Adm A.G. Kirk at left of photo.*

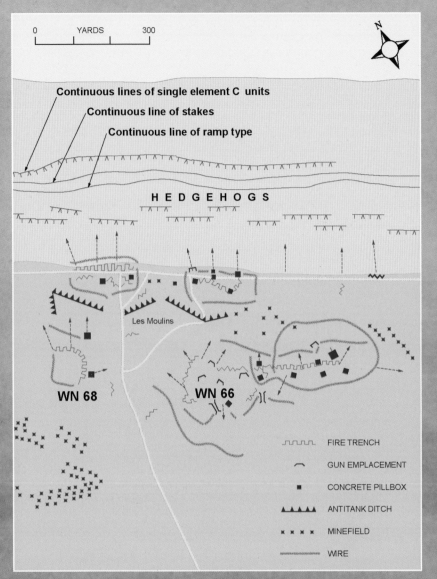

0   YARDS   300

N

Continuous lines of single element C units

Continuous line of stakes

Continuous line of ramp type

H E D G E H O G S

Les Moulins

WN 68

WN 66

ᴧᴧᴧᴧ	FIRE TRENCH
⌒	GUN EMPLACEMENT
■	CONCRETE PILLBOX
▲▲▲▲▲	ANTITANK DITCH
✕ ✕ ✕ ✕	MINEFIELD
⌇⌇⌇⌇⌇	WIRE

189988

Above: *LCVPs land 1st Bn/16th Inf Regt on Easy Red beach from USS* Samuel Chase *in the second wave around 07:30.*

Opposite, above: *A explosion, possibly a mine, catches the attention of sailors on Easy Red.*

Opposite, inset: *Big Red One cloth badge.*

Right: *Aerial view of Easy Red Beach just west of E-1 at about 12:00 on June 6. It shows the landing of the 18th and 115th Inf Regt. At the bottom of the picture is the anti-tank trench dug to protect WN 65.*

Below: *WN 64 was unfinished on June 6. It was taken by 2–Lt John M. Spaulding who won the DSC. This photo shows the view over Easy Red from WN 64.*

114

This 50mm anti-tank gun (**above**) in Type 677 casemate proved to be one of the most effective elements of the WN 65 strong-point covering the E-1 St Laurent draw. It was finally silenced by 37mm automatic cannon fire from a pair of M15A1 multiple gun motor carriage halftracks of the 467th AAA Battalion. Today it has a plaque honoring that unit (visible **top**).

Above right: The E-1 draw today. The bunker is identified at A; the 2nd Inf Div memorial (see opposite caption) at B.

Center right: Reinforcements flood onto Easy Red, the infantry making their way up the bluff by a path that ran behind the bunker (see opposite).

116

Right: Vehicles follow the E-1 exit road to St Laurent. Note the M16 GMC armed with quad .50s in foreground.

Above: *The Provisional Engineer Special Group used the bunker as an HQ and their exploits readying the beach for troop movements were remembered in the first plaque to be placed on the bunker.*

Above: *The follow-up troops of 2nd Inf Div move past the bunker on June 7. Today (as identified at B on modern photo) there is an obelisk to the division.*

Below: *The Gooseberry breakwater is in place, so this photo of Easy Red beach dates from mid-June 1944. The house is characteristic of so many photos of Easy Red.*

Opposite: *E-3 draw today, highlighting:*
A *WN 61 on west side of draw.*
B *The Big Red One memorial. To its left are the trenches shown* **opposite, below left** *The memorial (also shown on page 100) stands just above WN 62, the largest defensive position on Omaha, sited some 100ft above the beach. It was manned by men of 716th and 352nd Inf Divs, and artillery observers from a battery of 105mm artillery inland at Houtteville. Among its personnel was Gefreiter Heinrich Severloh—the "Beast of Omaha"—whose biography talked of him firing over 12,000 rounds, killing hundreds.*
C *WN 62 included two H669 casemates, the view of the beaches from one is shown* **opposite, below right**. *Today the 5th ESB memorial is placed on top of this bunker (***opposite, bottom right***). There are also plaques for the 299th, 146th, and the 20th Engineer Combat Bns, and lower down, for Canadian Navy minesweepers.*
D *US cemetery at Colleville.*

Above right: *LCIs 430 and 496 try to find a cleared channel to Fox Green beach.*

Right: *USS* LCI(L)L-85 *was manned by the USCG. It sank on June 6 at 14:30. Its after action report tells a graphic story. "At 08:20 we arrived at the line of departure. The primary control vessel for Easy Red beach called to us by loud hailer and told us to go into the beach at this point. As a result of the strong tide running along the beach … we actually landed in the left flank of Easy Red … rather than the right as scheduled." Having grounded at 08:30 they discovered the water was too deep to offload so backed out and tried again. "As the ship grounded a teller mine exploded under the bow … The port ramp went down and the troops began going ashore. Shells and machine gun fire began to hit us. About 50 troops got down the port ramp before a shell hit it and blew it off the sponsons and over the side. As the starboard ramp had not gone down and the wounded men were jamming the deck, we backed off the beach again." They had 15 dead and 30 wounded men and had been hit about 25 times by shells. Fire was starting in troop compartments and water was coming in from shell holes below the water line and the hole made by the mine. "We backed off the beach … The damage control party began fighting the fires and within 30 minutes had them out." LCVPs took off most of the remaining troops and* LCI(L)L-85, *by now listing badly, headed back to USS* Samuel Chase *to unload the casualties. Having done so, while trying to pump the boat out, she capsized and sank.*

Below right: *Looking toward Fox Green later in the day.*

Above and Right: *The east end of Omaha is recognizable for its cliffs, and many of 16th Inf Regt landed there rather than on Fox Green because of the current. Reinforced by other troops, they attacked and took WN 60 from which this view west was taken (**opposite, above**). Draw F-1 is in the foreground.*

Right: *Back for more! LST-603 launched four DD Shermans from B/741st Tank Bn and later returned, this time to Fox Green, to land jeeps from 16th Inf Regt and 32nd Fd Arty.*

120

Opposite, below: *The proximity between Omaha and Gold beaches is shown by this photo from the Big Red One Memorial. In the distance is the remains of Mulberry B off Arromanches.*

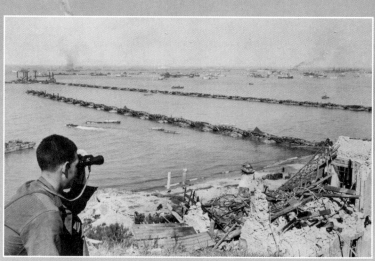

Opposite: *Mulberry A before the storm. Constructed by Seebees of the 108th Construction Bn, the gooseberry was completed by D+4, as was the first whale roadway. By D+12, over 310,000 men had reached France, many of them via this mulberry.*

This page: *In the early morning of July 19 the winds got up and waves of 12ft were experienced. Vessels were ripped from their moorings and hit the structure, damaging it seriously—as can be seen in these June 21 photos. Mulberry A was never rebuilt.*

Above: *Setting out from Omaha on June 8, the main task of 29th Div was to take Isigny. As part of this operation they took the Maisy Battery. Since then, the battery became overgrown and lost. However, today it is the scene of a remarkable transformation thanks to excavation by owner Gary Sterne. The guns—four 105mm and six 155mm—were heavily bombed on the night of June 5/6. This didn't stop the battery opening fire on D-Day; a naval bombardment followed but did not silence them. On the morning of June 9, the defenders were attacked by 2nd and 5th Rangers, soldiers from the 116th Inf Regt (29th Div), and 81st Chemical Weapons Bn (mortars). It was eventually captured by the 5th Rangers.*

Right: *Type 622 bunker at the battery.*

Above and Left: *Isigny, on the River Aure, was badly damaged in 1944—over 60 percent of its buildings were destroyed, mainly by naval fire, as can be seen in the contemporary photo. In 1944 it was the key to the junction with VII Corps. The 29th Div, the 175th Regt, with two companies of the 747th Tank Bn attached, advanced there via la Cambe (now the location of the German ceme-tery; see page 189). Arriving in the early hours of June 9 the bridge over the Aure was taken intact, and by 05:00, infantry and tanks were cleaning the houses of snipers; a weak enemy counter-attack was stopped and some 200 prisoners were taken.*

CHAPTER 7

GOLD BEACH

Follow-up troops land on Gold Beach on June 7. Note the disabled Sexton SP gun with the TT symbol of 50th (Northumbrian) Inf Div. Carrying a 25pdr, Sextons were built in Canada first on the Ram and later the Grizzly (Canadian-built M4A1) chassis. The TT symbol reflected the recruiting area for the division—between the rivers Tyne and Tees.

"To construct our defences we had in two years used some 13 million cubic meters of concrete and 1.5 million tons of steel. A fortnight after the landings by the enemy, this costly effort was brought to nothing because of an idea of simple genius."

Albert Speer talks about the Mulberry harbors

VER SUR MER

MONT FLEURY
BATTERY (WN 35A)

anti-tank ditch

WN 34

LA RIVIÈRE

WN 33

King Red Beach

Love Green Beach

WN 36

Jig

WN 35

Jig Red Beach

reen Beach

Gold Beach was allocated to the British Second Army's XXX Corps, with H-Hour set at 07:25. The assault was to be made by 50th (Northumbrian) Inf Div, which had been reinforced with 56th (Ind) Inf Bde, and was supported by the 8th Armd Bde. 50th's primary objective was to seize Bayeux, the Caen-Bayeux road, and the port of Arromanches; the secondary objectives, to make contact with the Americans at Omaha to the west and the Canadians landing at Juno to the east. The 231st Inf Bde, followed by the 56th Inf Bde, landed in the west, with DD tanks from the Nottinghamshire Yeomanry (Sherwood Rangers) in support. The assault battalions were the 1st Bn, Hampshire Regt on Jig Green (west side) and the 1st Bn, Dorset Regt on Jig Green (east side). The 69th Inf Bde, followed by 151st Inf Bde, landed in the east with DD tanks from the 4th/7th RDG in support. The assault battalions here were the 5th Bn, East Yorkshire Regt on King Red and the 6th Bn, Green Howards on King Green. The secret of the DD tanks had been well kept: the Germans didn't expect them. However, sea conditions in the sector were too rough and so they launched closer to the shore. Nevertheless, 4/7 RDG lost five and the Sherwood Rangers eight in the breakers. When night fell, the advance had reached the outskirts of Bayeux, Arromanches had been captured, and 47 Cdo was outside Port-en-Bessin (see page 145).

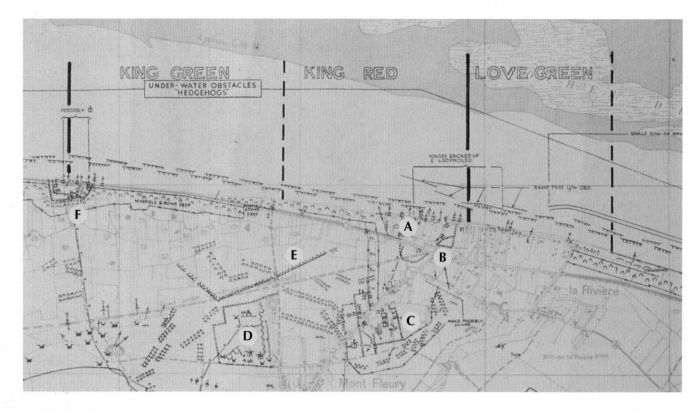

Above: *Wartime operational map showing:*

A *Location of WN 33 (see opposite).*

B *Today, this crossroads is where the Sexton (**right**) is located. It was put there as a memorial by the son of Capt Robert Kiln, 341st Bty, 86th (Hertfordshire Yeomanry) Fd Regt, RA.*

C *Location of WN 34.*

D *Location of the Fleury Battery—four 122mm Russian guns, two housed in Type 679 casemates; see page 139.*

E *Anti-tank ditch.*

F *Location of WN 35 at Hable de Heurlot.*

Below: *King Red photographed by a 10th PRG P-38 Lightning.*

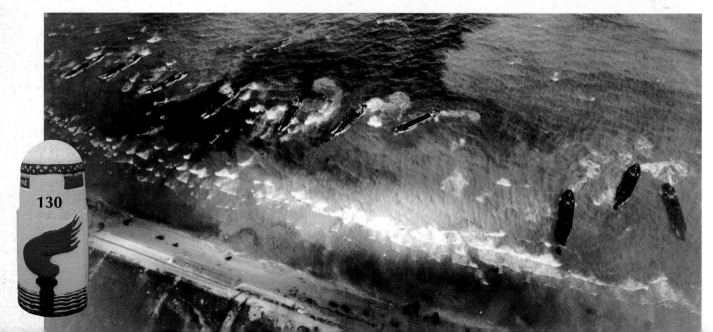

Right: *By the end of the war there were over 650,000 German prisoners in the UK, each graded by political conviction. The "black" ones—ideological Nazis—went to northern or Scottish PoW camps.*

Below: *Aerial view of King Beach showing clearly the results of bombing/naval bombardments and the scars of anti-tank ditches.The yellow rectangle shows the rough area of the photo opposite, below, of the gun battery at Mont Fleury. Three of its four casemates were under construction on June 6. Its four 122mm Polish guns were manned by 1260th GHQ Coastal Artillery Battalion. It was captured by 6th Battalion, The Green Howards, whose memorial at Crépon, south-west of another battery at WN 32, is shown on page 134.*

Opposite, above left: *A Cromwell Mk V tank of 4th County of London Yeomanry, 22nd Armd Bde, 7th Armd Div, leads a column of armor (including a Sherman Firefly immediately behind) and other vehicles inland from Gold Beach, on June 7. Interestingly, this Cromwell—T121766W—was one of those knocked out by Wittmann on June 13 during the action at Villers Bocage.*

Opposite, above right and inset: *CSM Stanley Hollis, Green Howards, was the only winner of the Victoria Cross on D-Day. The citation for his award says: "Wherever fighting was heaviest CSM Hollis appeared, and in the course of a magnificent day's work he displayed the utmost gallantry, and on two separate occasions his courage and initiative prevented the enemy from holding up the advance at critical stages. It was largely through his heroism and resource that the company's objectives were gained and casualties were not heavier and, by his own bravery, he saved the lives of many of his men." Inset is the Stanley Hollis Hut (at **A** in the photo **right**) which was bought by The Green Howards in 2005 and renovated as a memorial. A tramstop shelter, it was mistaken for a pillbox on June 6.*

TANK TRAPS

A

Order of Battle

50th (Northumbrian) Inf Div

69th Bde
5th Bn, East Yorkshire Regt
6th and 7th Bn, Green
  Howards

151st Bde
6th, 8th, and 9th Bn Durham
  Light Infantry

231st Bde
2nd Bn, Devonshire Regt
1st Bn, Hampshire Regt
1st Bn, Dorsetshire Regt

Divisional Troops
61st Recce Regt, RAC
50th Div Engr
50th Div Sigs
74th, 90th, and 124th Fd,
  102nd A/Tk, and 25th LAA
  Regts, RA
2nd Bn Cheshire Regt (MG)

Attached
56th Ind Inf Bde (2nd Bn, South
  Wales Borderers; 2nd Bn,
  Essex Regt; 2nd Bn, Glouces-
  tershire Regt)
8th Armd Bde (4th/7th Royal
  Dragoon Guards; 24th
  Lancers; Nottinghamshire
  Yeomanry; 12th Bn, King's
  Royal Rifle Corps)
86th and 174th Fd Regts RA
  detached from Corps Troops
  (SP guns)
No 47 (RM) Commando
Two squadrons from 6th
  Assault Regt, RE
1 RM Armd Support Regt
89th and 90th Fd Coys, RE

Above: This aerial photograph shows the German strongpoint at WN 35 (at **A**) soon after its capture. Note the three tanks in the center of the strongpoint the vehicles and personnel on the beach and coast road and the track inland towards the Mont Fleury Battery.

Left: This Green Howards memorial was unveiled at Crépon by HM Harold V, King of Norway, in 1996 (his father and grandfather were both colonel-in-chief of the regiment).

Below: Soldiers of the 7th Green Howards cross King Green beach at about 08:30. An 81st Assault Squadron AVRE fitted with a Bobbin mat-layer is visible in the surf towards the right of the photograph, as are beach obstacles (by this time becoming submerged as the tide somes in), Sherman tanks and other vehicles.

Above: LCT(R)-440 *supported 69th Brigade's assault on King Beach. A single LCT(R) could carry over a thousand RP-3 60lb rockets of the same type as those used by the Hawker Typhoons. The drenching effect of the rockets in a small area significantly demoralized enemy troops at crucial moments. First used—with great success— during the Sicily landings, they were used on both British and US D-Day beaches.*

Left: *A variety of vehicles on King Green—Sherman tanks, Universal carriers and an AVRE "Bobbin" mat-layer*

Below: *DD tanks from the 4th/7th Royal Dragoon Guards, supporting 69th Brigade, advancing near Rucqueville on the morning of June 7.*

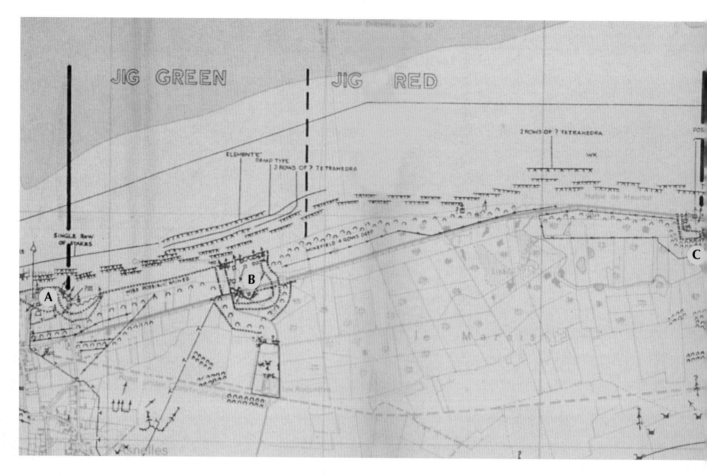

Above: *Operational map of Jig sector of Gold Beach, showing:*
A *WN 37 at Le Hamel. The defensive position at the Sanatorium had a 612 casemate with a 75mm FK gun. It was taken by the Hampshires on the afternoon of D-Day after hard fighting which saw its 75mm knock out a number of British tanks.*
B *WN 36, with a casemated 50mm KwK, was called the "Customs House" and was also stormed by the Hampshires.*
C *WN 35 at Hable de Heuriot was finally attacked and defeated by tanks of the 6th Green Howards supported by AVREs of 6th Assault Regt, RE.*

Opposite, below: *Monument in memory of 2nd Bn, the South Wales Borderers who landed at Asnelles. The only Welsh battalion to land with the assault troops on D-Day, It went in at Le Hamel as part of the second wave, and pushed inland to the high ground north of Bayeux.*

Opposite, above: *Men of 47 Commando come ashore from LCIs and head for Port-en-Bessin (see page 145).*

136

Left: *An armoured bulldozer of British 8th Armd Bde clears the beach so that tanks can land from a landing craft. A conventional Caterpillar D7 bulldozer fitted with armor to protect the driver and the engine, this was one of "Hobart's Funnies" operated by the 79th Armd Div.*

Above: *This Vf600 with its pedestal-mounted 50mm gun is very similar to the one found at at Le Hamel (**above right**) and at St Aubin-sur-Mer on Juno Beach (see page 160). The strength of the back wall meant these emplacements were rarely knocked out from behind.*

Above right: *The field of fire of this Vf600e at WN 37 in Le Hamel shows why it was so effective.*

Opposite, above: *The casemate at WN 37 proved a very tough nut to crack. There is some dispute as to whether it housed an 88mm or 75mm gun—but there's no disputing that it knocked out a number of tanks and was only subdued in the afternoon of June 6 after having been hit at close range by a Churchill AVRE's Petard. The plaque on it identifies that the killer blow was supplied by a 25pdr SP gun of the Essex Yeomanry commanded by Sgt R.E. Palmer, MM. It was supported by two more 75mm guns in WN 39, high up on the hill above Le Hamel on the way to Arromanches (see page 141).*

Right: *USCG-manned LST-21 transported elements of 56th Ind Inf Bde attached to 50th (Northumbrian) Inf Div to Jig Green from Southampton. The Sherman named* Virgin *was part of HQ 8th Ind Armd Bde; the lorry on the left is from the Nottinghamshire Yeomanry (Sherwood Rangers).*

Above: X marks the spot on the hill outside Arromanches where Eric Bates met up with his unit. Now it's a viewing platform: compare with photo opposite. The circular building (**Y**) houses Arromanches 360, a panoramic cinema.

Left: Sgt. Eric Bates in 1944; today he's a sprightly nonagenarian.

Below: A five-man 40mm crew ready to fire. (1) gun commander; (2) ammo handler; (3) one of two layers; (4) gunner. Note (5) the four-round clip; (6) the Stiffkey Sight to provide the correct lead on the target, and (6) spare ammo at rear of C9/B.

Sgt Eric Bates had served with ADGB on 3.7-inch guns until his unit was disbanded in 1943 and he joined 395th/120th LAA Regt, RA. 395th Battery was equipped with a "Carrier, 30 cwt, SP, 4x4, 40mm AA (Bofors)"—a 40mm gun mounted on a Morris-Commercial C9/B chassis. In May 1944, after months of training, his unit moved to Leyton, SE London, spending a week surrounded by barbed wire in a well-policed compound waterproofing their vehicles. Then they marched through the town, receiving the well wishes of the populace (Give 'em hell boys!), to the Port of London where they embarked on a Liberty ship. The ship anchored off Southend for a day (when D-Day was postponed) and then hastened through the Dover Straits around the time that the Liberty ship SS Sambut was hit and sunk by German shelling, but his vessel made it through safely. He discovered his destination when, around 02:00 on June 6, his battery officer told them about the invasion and each was handed a copy of Eisenhower's letter. A few hours later, netting was thrown over the side of the ship and he cautiously made his way down—amid the catcalls of the troops at the railings—to the LCT Mk 4 below. There, four of his battery's six C9/Bs were waiting. Around midday, they were off. He had had no training for a seaborne assault; he had never been on a landing craft before; he hadn't been given a map; indeed, he remembers that he didn't even know where Normandy was! As he waited in his vehicle, an American sailor (USCG manned a number of landing craft used by British forces) told him that he was the first off and that he should go right so that, if his vehicle stalled or was hit, the ramp was clear for the next vehicle. On went the engines and suddenly the ramp was lowered. He gunned the engine, drove down the ramp, landing in a foot of water. Then he was through the surf and onto the shingle: he had arrived on Jig Beach. Sgt Bates followed the instructions of, first, the beachmasters, then MPs along his route (having got there on their "Clockwork Mouse" James 125cc motorcycles), stopping only to remove the tin can he had placed on top of his waterproofed engine air intake. His battery moved east, without seeing the enemy, to the top of the hill above Arromanches where they met the other two vehicles and the rest of their battery (shipped on other vessels). They were deployed—as they found out later—as air protection for the construction of Mulberry B, although they had little to do there. The only scare was when they moved to Port-en-Bessin on D+4 to set up a defensive position when they were told 21st Panzer would be attacking (luckily, this didn't happen). Their heaviest labor was to provide assistance on Arromanches beach to unload DUKWs. Apart from the occasional barrage (15 rounds fired to a set location to dissuade German aircraft in the area), they had no occasion to fire their weapons in anger.

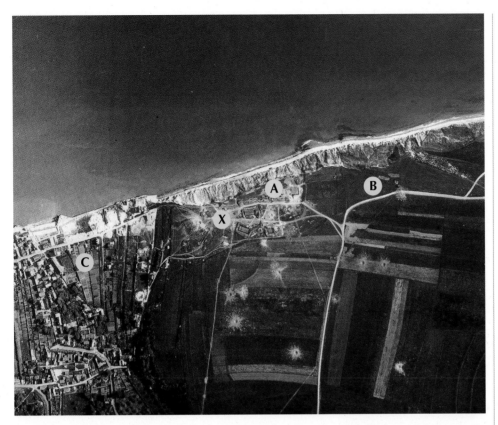

Left: *WN 38 (**A**) and WN 39 (**B**) can be clearly seen in the center of this June 4 aerial photograph. Arromanches is at **C** and to the right, out of the picture, are the Gold beaches, Asnelles, and Le Hamel. WN 39 was tasked with providing fire onto Gold Beach and was the objective of D Coy, 1st Hampshires who captured the strongpoint about 15:20 on June 6. **X** marks the spot where Eric Bates met up with his unit—near the radar station.*

Below left: *Diagram of Mulberry B near Arromanches. Note the roadways leading from the "Spud" pierheads, so-called because of their four feet or spuds. The roadways reached up to 0.75 miles from shore, resting on floating pontoons nicknamed "beetles."*

Below: *Another view of Mulberry B—by now nicknamed Port Winston—this one on October 2.*
A *LST Pier.*
B *An extra row of caissons has been added to help protect the blockships against the weather . Each day around 9,000 tons were landed via Mulberry B until the end of August by which time Cherbourg port became available for use—at least in part—and, towards the end of the year, after the capture of Walcheren, the port of Antwerp. Mulberry B was in use for 5 months during which time over 2 million men, half a million vehicles and 4 million tons of supplies passed through the harbor.*

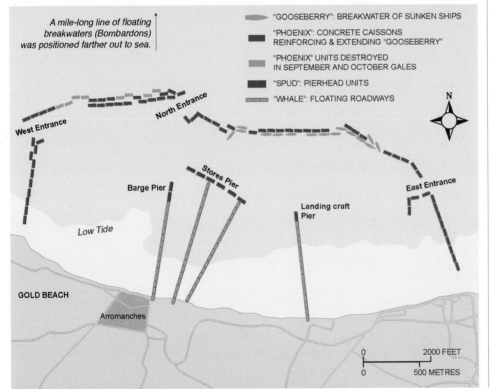

A mile-long line of floating breakwaters (Bombardons) was positioned farther out to sea.

"GOOSEBERRY": BREAKWATER OF SUNKEN SHIPS

"PHOENIX": CONCRETE CAISSONS REINFORCING & EXTENDING "GOOSEBERRY"

"PHOENIX" UNITS DESTROYED IN SEPTEMBER AND OCTOBER GALES

"SPUD": PIERHEAD UNITS

"WHALE": FLOATING ROADWAYS

West Entrance

North Entrance

Stores Pier

Barge Pier

Landing craft Pier

East Entrance

Low Tide

GOLD BEACH

Arromanches

N

0   2000 FEET
0   500 METRES

Left: *Arromanches today.*
A *The excellent Musée du Debarquement.*
B *Point where the center roadway reached land, Place du 6 Juin.*
C *A number of roadway supporting "Beetles" still can be seen on the beach.*
D *One of two 612 casemates that defended Arromanches. This one has above it an M4A2 Sherman, named Berry au Bac, of Gen Leclerc's 2nd Armored Division as a memorial.*

Above and Top: *The central roadway reaches land. Mulberry B was constructed by Nos 969 and 970 Port Floating Equipment Coys, with the on-land assistance coming from the RE.*

The battery at Longues—WN 48—is an impressive reminder of the strength of the Atlantic Wall, although its performance on June 6 reflected many of the problems, too. Completed in 1944, it was built and manned by German Naval troops although under German Army control. The four 152mm guns, housed in M272 casemates, posed a significant threat to the Allied forces, and so it was bombed heavily—1,500 tons were dropped on the night of June 5/6 (although most hit the nearby village) and from 05:37 on the 6th it was bombarded by the French cruiser Georges Leygues *and USS* Arkansas. *This didn't stop the battery itself opening fire at 06:05 and managing 170 shots before it was effectively silenced by British cruisers* Ajax *and* Argonaut, *although a single gun operated intermittently until 19:00. The problem was that none of the shots fired by the battery were accurate. The telephone link to the M262 fire control bunker (***above***) was cut by the bombing and the crew of the battery (184 men, half of them over 40 years old) had little training. It surrendered to the British 231st Inf Bde on the 7th. See also photos on pages 2–3 and 21.*

144

Port-en-Bessin was captured by 47 RM Commando in a great feat of arms. The unit landed 12 miles away on Gold Beach, infiltrated enemy lines, and made their way to the port. The commandos had lost around a quarter of their anticipated strength—4 of their 14 LCAs were sunk (3 by mines 1 by shellfire); they lost 40 casualties at Le Hamel; and after leaving Jig Green east they lost 12 more en route, some to MGs at La Rosière. They got through the outer defenses and headed into the port when they were spotted. The Germans had two Flak ships in the harbor and soon 11 men had been killed, 17 wounded, and two captured. HMS Emerald and rocket-firing Typhoons took care of the Flak ships and on the evening of June 7, when dark fell, Capt Terence Cousins, who died in the attack, led 25 men up the hill and charged the enemy bunkers. The defenders, from 352nd Div, surrendered. Before the Mulberry harbors were built, Port-en-Bessin became an important point for resupply of petrol via a smaller version of PLUTO which ran from a tanker berthing point to the town.

Above: Aerial view of Port-en-Bessin after the great storm in mid-June (note the two ships ashore at **A**).

Below: The town today.
A The 1694 Vauban tower used as an ammo store.
B WN 56: casemate for a 57mm gun.
C Commando memorial
D WN 57 two casemates for 57mm Skoda guns.

Left: A Universal Carrier disembarks alongside the harbor jetty, on June 10. WN 57's clifftop pillbox is visible on the right. The four buildings nearest the camera survive today (as can be seen below). Port-en-Bessin doubled as Ouistreham in the movie The Longest Day.

CHAPTER 8

JUNO BEACH

"At the end of the day, its forward elements stood deeper into France than those of any other division. The opposition the Canadians faced was stronger than that of any other beach save Omaha. That was an accomplishment in which the whole nation could take considerable pride."

John Keegan in *Overlord*

Assault landing craft from HMCS Prince David *and SS* Monowai *during their run in to Nan White Beach on D-Day.*

On D-Day, the 3rd Canadian Infantry Division landed on Juno Beach and performed admirably. They faced strong defenses but by the end of the day they had advanced further into France than either the British or American forces. They suffered significant casualties: nearly a third of the landing craft that launched were destroyed or damaged, most by mines, and there were nearly a thousand casualties, including 340 dead—21,400 men had landed and were well-placed to resist the German counterattacks which came on the 7th. Two infantry brigades assaulted: 7th Inf Bde with 6th Armd Regt on Mike and Nan Green beaches around Courseulles-sur-Mer; and 8th Inf Bde with 10th Armd Regt on Nan White and Red between Bernières and St. Aubin. Also involved was 48 RM Cdo, which landed on Nan Red, with the mission of taking the strong-point at Langrune and then effecting a linkup with 41 Cdo and the western edge of the Sword beaches.

7th Inf Bde was spearheaded on Mike Green and Red by the Royal Winnipeg Rifles, an assault company of the Canadian Scottish Regt, and one squadron of the 1st Hussars. On Nan Green, the Regina Rifle Regt were supported by another 1st Hussars squadron. The reserve troops of the Winnipeg Rifles and Canadian Scottish Regiment landed shortly after and the attack pushed into Couseulles.

On Nan White and Red, 8th Inf Bde's Queen's Own Rifles of Canada and North Shore Regt had a more difficult time, sustaining casualties from direct fire and mines on the shore. The tanks of the Fort Garry Horse, assisted by AVREs of 80th Assault Sqn, RE helped subdue the strongpoint. The reserve battalion, Le Régiment de la Chaudière, and 48 Cdo deployed next, the latter sustaining over 150 casualties. Problems on Nan Red meant that the followup troops—9th Inf Bde (Cameron Highlanders of Ottawa, the North Nova Scotia Highlanders, the Stormont, Dundas and Glengarry Highlanders, and the Highland Light Infantry of Canada) and 27th Armd Regt—had to land in Bernières and Nan White. This led to a huge traffic jam on the beach and slowed up progress, but soon the advance was underway and the Canadian troops surged forward.

Right: *The Juno Beach Centre, designed by architect Brian K. Chamberlain, was inaugurated on June 6, 2003. This statue entitled Remembrance and Renewal," stands between the museum and the dunes.*

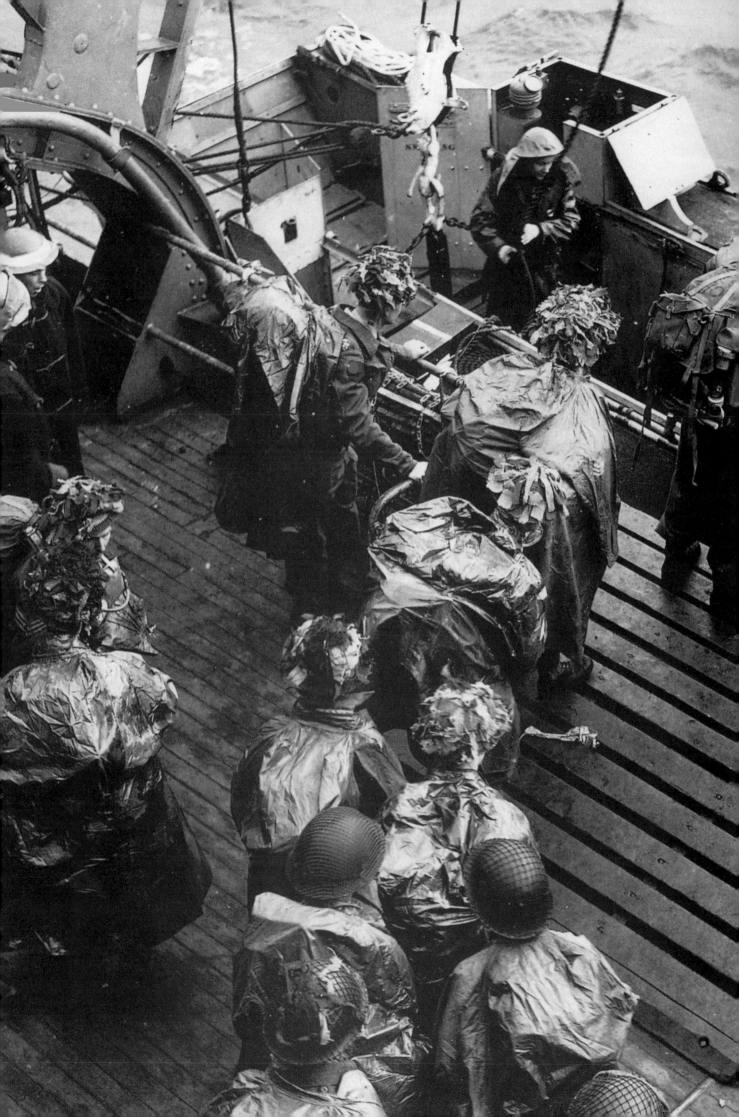

C

Left: *Courseulles-sur-Mer today is a bustling town with a modern marina and very much changed from the way it looked in 1944. Little remains of the strongpoints that defended the coastline here. Mike Red Beach is to the right of the picture; Nan Green to the left. At **A** is the Juno Beach Centre; **B** the "Remembrance and Renewal" statue; **C** one of the DD tanks (also see page 153) lost on June 6 which was recovered in 1970 and restored. Badges of units who fought in the area are welded to it.*

Below, left to right: *Three views of the harbor entrance and estuary of the River Seulles at Courseulles. The left picture was taken on the afternoon of D-Day with the tide half out. The earlier high tide has allowed two large tank landing ships to beach near the high water mark at the top of Mike Red Beach; the second (**center**) view shows a similar location with more vessels; the final (**right**) image shows armor moving off the beach through Lane M2 (Yellow Gap)—to the west of WN 31—which had been opened by 2nd Tp, 26th Assault Regt.*

Above: *This oblique aerial view shows Mike Red Beach in front of the meandering Seulles. Note the inundation in the background: the Germans had forced many of the rivers in the area to flood. On the right of the river 7th Bde Gp land in front of WN 31; at left, the burning buildings are in front of WN 29.*

Right: *Crew from 3rd Anti-Tank Regt, RCA remove waterproofing from their M10 Wolverine after arriving over Mike Red Beach.*

Below right: *The DD tank was recovered in 1970 as the sign next to it explains.*

Opposite, above: *What can be seen of WN 31 is just to the right of the Cross of Lorraine. The latter was placed there in 1990 to commemorate Charles de Gaulle's landing in France on June 14.*

Opposite, center: *Map showing the Canadian assault on Juno and subsequent advance.*

Opposite, below: *Infantrymen of the 1st Battalion, the Royal Winnipeg Rifles, in LCAs en route to land at Mike Red. First, B Company landed at the western edge of Courseulles; then D Company landed and moved to the west to take Graye-sur-Mer. A and C Companies were in reserve but landed while the beaches were still under fire. They landed before their supporting tanks—of 1st Hussars—and RE vehicles which were delayed by navigational error.*

JUNO BEACH

At 0730 hours 6th June 1944, the 6th Canadian Armoured Regiment (First Hussars) in support of the 7 Canadian Infantry Brigade of the 3 Canadian Infantry Division, assaulted and overpowered enemy defences between Courseulles-sur-Mer and Bernieres-sur-Mer. This tank, recovered from the sea nearly 27 years after launching, is dedicated by the First Hussars to the memory of all who participated in this operation.

DUPLEX DRIVE (DD) TANK

The Duplex Drive Sherman Tank had a waterproof chassis fitted with a collapsible canvas screen and rubber tubes inflated with air. It was moved through the water by two propellors at the rear, and on reaching shore reverted to a normal tank.

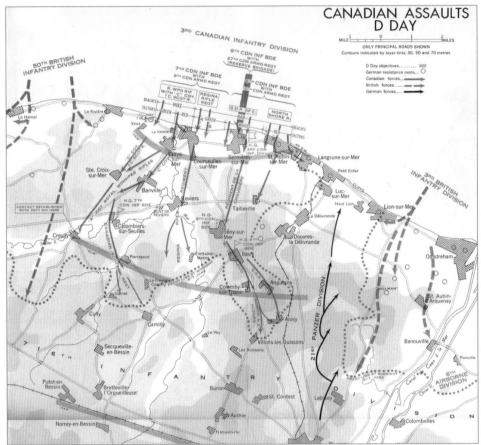

CANADIAN ASSAULTS D DAY

3RD CANADIAN INFANTRY DIVISION

ONLY PRINCIPAL ROADS SHOWN
Contours indicated by layer-tints: 30, 50 and 70 metres

D Day objectives..........
German resistance nests...
Canadian forces.....
British forces.....
German forces.....

Order of Battle

Canadian 3rd Inf Div

7th Bde
Royal Winnipeg Rifles
Regina Rifles
1st Bn, Canadian Scottish Regt

8th Bde
Queen's Own Rifles of Canada
Le Régiment de la Chaudière
North Shore (New Brunswick)
  Regt

9th Bde
Highland Light Infantry
Stormont, Dundas, and Glen-
  garry Highlanders
North Nova Scotia
  Highlanders

Divisional Troops
7th Recce Regt (17th Duke of
  York's Royal Canadian
  Hussars)
3rd Canadian Div Engr
3rd Canadian Div Sigs
12th, 13th, and 14th Fd, 3rd
  A/Tk, and 4th LAA Regts,
  RCA
Cameron Highlanders of
  Ottawa (MG)

2nd Armd Bde
6th Armd Regt (1st Hussars)
10th Armd Regt (Fort Garry
  Horse)
27th Armd Regt
  (Sherbrooke Fusiliers Regt)

Right: *This crowded scene looks west toward Courseulles-sur-Mer from the eastern end of Nan Green Beach on the afternoon of June 6. Engineers of the beach groups (note white bands round helmets) work on the roadway and at right there's a bulldozer, probably an armored D7, helping. A 2nd Armd Bde Sherman III waits to leave the beach. The troops disembarking are from 7th Inf Bde.*

Below right: *Another view of Nan Green looking past the stern of LCT Mk 4 575 toward Courseulles—a very much smaller town than it is today.*

Below, left and right: *WN 29 was a extremely strong defensive position with 88mm, 75mm, and 50mm guns, and a number of MG positions. As the right-hand photo shows, the field of fire extended over Mike beaches. WN 29 caused many casualties to the Regina Rifles and 1st Hussar DDs who landed nearby. It was only finally taken after a bitter battle, when these troops were assisted by Centaurs of 2nd RM Armd Support Regt using their 95mm weapons at close range. Once taken, the attackers sited a 20mm AA position on top of the Type 677 88mm casemate.*

Left: *A Centaur IV of 2nd RM Armd Support Regt with its deep wading hood still attached, pulling a Porpoise ammo sled. Used as artillery for "drenching" fire on the run-in to the beach to keep the enemy's heads down, the Centaur IV's 95mm gun proved very useful in bunker busting. Some 26 Centaurs and 7 Sherman artillery OP tanks landed on D-Day, with another 4 + 1 on D+1.*

Below left: *The defenses long since neutralized, Canadian troops make their way off the beach toward Courseulles.*

Below: *Looking past the deep wading hood of a Stuart V, this view over the sandy beach between Bernières et Courseulles shows a mass of men and vehicles including a Humber 4x4 in the center and a file of Sherman IIIs on the right.*

Above: *Follow-up troops arrive on Juno. To the left is the hulk of LCA-519, destroyed on June 6; to the right LCT Mk 3 474 of 11th LCT Flotilla. Landing craft have sterns with a deeper draft than the bows so that they can run further onto the beach. Reversing off is trickier. To help, the LCIs dropped a large stern anchor on the final run in and used a rear winch, visible in this photo, to pull the craft off the beach. Note just behind the walking soldiers the beach obstacles that have been gathered for disposal by navy beach parties.*

Below: *Gib Milne's photo of LCI-125 from LCI-306. 125 carried A Coy and 1st Pl, D Coy of the Highland Light Infantry who had only a short paddle onto French soil with their bicycles.*

Inset: *The Highland Light Infantry of Canada aboard LCI(L) 306 of the 2nd Canadian (262nd RN) Flotilla lands at Bernières-sur-Mer on June 6 with the rest of 9th Inf Bde. Wallace McQuade's photo includes Gib Milne taking pictures from the bow gun platform.*

Above and Below: *Two of the classic views of HMCS LCI(L)-299 of the 2nd Canadian (262nd RN) Flotilla on Nan White Beach on June 6 taken by Gib Milne. For many years identified as being Highland Light Infantry, the troops of 9th Inf Bde disembarking are in fact from the Stormont, Dundas, and Glengarry Regt. LCI(L)-299 has beached in relatively deep water so the troops had to wade.*

Right: *Maj-Gen Rod Keller was General Officer Commanding the Canadian 3rd Inf Div, and on D-Day led by example. He left Normandy after being wounded on August 8, a victim of a friendly fire incident when US bombers hit Canadian troops during Operation Tractable.*

Above: *Cpl Victor Deblois of Le Régiment de la Chaudière guarding German prisoners on Nan White Beach. Note the anti-tank wall behind them.*

Below right: *The Maison de Queen's Own Rifles of Canada—more often called the Canadian House—is one of the most distinctive buildings on this stretch of coastline and still bears the scars of battle. A plaque in front of the house reads: "This house was liberated at first light on D-Day 6th June 1944, by the men of The Queen's Own Rifles of Canada who were the first Canadians to land on this beach. It may very well have been the first house on French soil liberated by seaborne Allied Forces. Within sight of this house over 100 men of The Queen's Own Rifles were killed or wounded, in the first few minutes of the landings." A visitor's book inside the house has an entry: "Ernie Kells, Queen's Own Rifles—one of five soldiers who arrived at this house on D-Day, now 84 years old. Sorry about throwing grenades into your cellar."*

Above and Opposite, center:
A marks the Canadian House on the Bernières-sur-Mer seafront. To its side is a liberation monument.
B Memorial commemorating the Canadians who died here on June 6. It is in the shape of an Inukshuk, a stone cairn roughly shaped like a person.

Left and Below left: A number of Canadian Army Film and Photo Unit photographers were working on D-Day, and Lt Ken Bell, who accompanied the Highland Light Infantry of Canada, shot the only color footage. This photo (**left**) shows troops disembarking at Bernières and heading inland. The Canadian House is in front of them and, in the distance, is the tower of the 13th century Church of Notre-Dame which suffered some damage during the battle (**below left**). Inside the church there is a stained-glass window donated by the son of Ernest W. Parker, Royal Signals, who landed on June 6 with QORC Regt.

Right and Opposite: *Two aerial views showing Nan White Beach at Bernières on June 6, 1944 and in 2013.*
A *marks a beach exit on today's rue du Royal Berkshire Régiment.*
B *shows the exit next to the Canadian House. In the 1944 photo a file of tanks heads north on the road today named rue du Regiment de la Chaudière.*
C *marks a Tobruk, part of WN 28, which was armed with an MG 08/15 and today sports a plaque to the QORC (also shown* **below right** *with prisoners from 5 Kp. II/Grenadier Regt 736/716 Inf Div).*
D *identifies the main WN 28 bunker, with a memorial to QORC and plaques to honor the Stormont, Dundas & Glengarry Highlanders; 5th Hackney Bn, the Royal Berkshire Regt; and No 3 Beach Group. Nearby are memorials to the Fort Garry Horse and La Chaudière Regiment.*
E *identifies another Tobruk.*

Below: *The eastern end of Juno, St Aubin-sur-Mer, was defended by WN 27 and its 50mm bunker, seen today. Assaulted by the two companies of the North Shore (New Brunswick) Regt, this strongpoint provided a resilient defense and knocked out two DD Shermans and two AVREs. It was only just after 11:00 that the area was taken. (See also pages 162–163.)*

Above: *The defensive fulcrum of Nan Red Beach was the 50mm bunker seen at **A** (and **below**). At **B** is the memorial to the North Shore Regt and 48 RM Cdo. The latter lost two LCIs to mines and more men in the fighting at St Aubin. There were too few of them left to take WN 26 at Langrune, and they and 41 Cdo from Sword were unable to link the bridgehead.*

Below: *This 1944 view of St Aubin looks from the 50mm bunker towards the town. The detritus on the beach below the high seawall includes a P-47 Thunderbolt that crash-landed on the beach and a Sherman DD, one of the tanks knocked out by the defenders who had fortified houses on the seafront to create the WN 27 strongpoint.*

Above: *St Aubin beach crowded with men of the North Shore Regt and 80th Assault Sqn armor: at left a D7 armored bulldozer; in the center a DD Sherman; at right, a BARV, another DD Sherman, and a Churchill AVRE.*

Left: *A frame from the classic CFPU film footage of the North Shore Regiment—probably A Coy—landing in front of Les Hirondelles between Bernières-sur-Mer and St Aubin on the left flank of Juno Beach. The troops wear the new P1944 Mk III "Turtle" helmets, introduced shortly before D-Day.*

Below: *Headquarters personnel of 4th SpS Bde, making their way from LCI(S)s onto Nan Red at St Aubin at about 09:00 on June 6.*

Left: *Le Régiment de la Chaudière was the only French-Canadian regiment involved in Overlord. It landed at Bernières-sur-Mer after the Queen's Own Rifles and although losing a number of landing craft and men to mines, by 10:30 was able to start advancing inland, supported by the armor of the Fort Garry Horse and 105mm SP Priests of the 14th Field Regt. By mid afternoon they had reached Colomby-sur-Thaon where today there's a stele of remembrance to the regiment.*

Below left: *Shermans moving through the narrow streets of Thaon on the drive inland from the beaches. Cleared of Germans by the 7th, the town was shelled regularly for some weeks afterward as the battle lines became static. Note the use of track links as appliqué armor—something that caught on quickly in Normandy. It may not have made any real improvement to protection, but as Michael McNorgan said in* The Gallant Hussars, *"They didn't care a hoot about fuel, track or engine wear; they cared about getting across the next one hundred yards of ground and living to tell the story. If the extra armor was not real protection, that didn't matter either, they liked it and if it helped their morale and gave them more confidence in their vehicles then it was worth the expense."*

Below: *The most powerful weapon in the Allied inventory was the 17pdr-equipped Sherman Firefly (a later nickname) one of which by June 1944 was allocated to each troop—this one, probably seen in July, named* Erich *by its crew. Often condemned by historians caught up in arguments about the effectiveness of Montgomery's attacks on Caen—and his unpleasant personality— the reality was that British and Canadian armor performed better than is appreciated in the difficult terrain of the bocage. 79th Armd Div's "Funnies"— particularly the AVREs and Crabs—did well on the beaches, and the attritional battles around Caen meant that by August there was little German armor in front of Operation Cobra when it happened.*

There were two significant armored counterattacks after D-Day: the 21st Panzer Division attacked the British in Sword sector on the 6th (see page 183) and the 12th SS Panzer Division (Hitlerjugend) was ordered to halt the Canadian advance. The first units of the 12th SS reached Evrecy at around 22:00 on the 6th and on the 7th attacked. They were led by Kurt Meyer's 25th SS PzGr Regt, with 50 PzKpfw IVs tanks of II/SS Pz Regt 12, and the artillery of III/SS Pz Regt 12.

Left: PzKpfw IV ausf H of 6./SS Pz Regt 12 on its way to the front. Note the Schürzen sideplates.

Below left: Panther ausf A of 3.I/SS Pz Regt 12 on the side of the road between Norrey-en-Bessin and Bretteville-l'Orgueilleuse. Attacking the Regina Rifle Regiment, the 3. Kompanie was ambushed by nine Shermans of C Sqn, 25th Armd Delivery Regt (the Elgin Regiment) who brought replacement tanks from Juno Beach. Seven Panthers were destroyed and 15 of 35 crewmen killed.

Bottom left and Below: This Panther ausf G of 4.I/SS Pz Regt 12, was knocked out by a PIAT team—Riflemen Joseph E. LaPointe and Gill A. Carnie and L/Cpl Clarence V. Hewitt—close to the Regina Rifles HQ in Bretteville-l'Orgueilleuse on June 8. The PIAT spring-launched a 2.5lb-bomb to an effective range of around 100 yards—but without smoke or anything to give the firing position away. It was remarkably efficient: 7% of German tanks knocked out by British and Canadian forces were knocked out by PIATs, although they were less effective when Schürzen were employed.

CHAPTER 9
SWORD BEACH

"He either fears his fate too much,
Or his deserts are small,
Who dare not put it to the touch,
To win or lose it all."

Monty's address to 21st Army Group troops on D-Day, quoting the Earl of Montrose

Medics deal with the dead and wounded in the shelter of an abandoned 79th Armd Div AVRE SBG carrier, whose bridge has been laid. The photo is opposite Lane 2 of Queen Red, near the "Cod" strongpoint that was finally quietened at around 10:00 on the 6th.

Early morning (08:00) aerial view of Sword Beach. This photo shows a USAAF Ninth Air Force B-26 Marauder aircraft and most likely LCAs and LCTs on the beach as part of Assault Group S-3 with the 8th Inf Bde. The split between Red and White beaches is shown by the dotted line. WN16 ("Morris") is just off the photo at upper left and WN 21 ("Trout") is at right in Lion-sur-Mer.

WN 16
MORRIS

WN 20
COD

COLLEVILLE
(MONTGOMERY)
PLAGE

WN 18

Red Beach

HERMANVILLE

LA BRÈCHE

White Beach

Sword was assaulted on a narrow front: two beaches, Red attacked by the East Yorkshires and White by the South Lancs. The assault was spearheaded by the DD tanks of the 13th/18th Hussars, who coped well with the waves, the maneuvering landing craft, and German defensive fire—23 of the 40 launched would survive the initial battle. The East Yorks made their way off the beach and took "Sole," "Trout," and "Daimler"—British designations of the German defensive positions used fish names for coastal and car types for inland sites. The main defensive location was "Cod," which was taken by the South Lancs after three hours of heavy fighting, allowing the next wave of troops to head inland, where 1st Suffolks took "Morris" and "Hillman; the rest of 185th Bde headed towards Caen, the Ulsters establishing a defensive position on the Periers Ridge high ground. At the extreme eastern edge of the landings, No 4 and 10th Inter-Allied Cdos landed and fought their way into Ouistreham, to take WN 10 and the Riva Bella strongpoint. The remainder of Lord Lovat's 1st SpS Bde moved inland to relieve the men of 6th Airborne Div at Pegasus Bridge and on the eastern side of the River Orne. They were joined there later the same day by the 2nd Warwicks and tanks of 27th Armd Bde. On the other flank, White Beach, 4th SpS Bde, spearheaded by No 41 Cdo, reached strongpoint "Trout," WN 21, which the enemy had vacated, but the nearby chateau was obdurately defended—so much so that 41 Cdo did not attack its secondary objective, the Douvres radar station.

EAST YORKSHIRE

170

Opposite, above and below: *Colleville-Montgomery-Plage is at the eastern edge of Queen Red Beach and was assaulted by the 2nd Bn, East Yorks Regt. Today it has a number of memorials to those who fought on June 6:*

A *General Montgomery statue. The town of Colleville-sur-Orne changed its name in 1946 to honor the commander of the Allied ground forces in 1944.*

B *WN 18 (also **below**) The main casemate housed an enfiladed 75mm gun. It was knocked out by tank fire at close range.*

C *No 4 Commando monument. This unit included the attached Free French 10 Cdo.*

D *Statue to Bill Millin, Lord Lovat's private piper, who played as 1st SpS Bde landed. After the war, interviewed German soldiers said they didn't shoot him because they thought he was mad!*

Above: *This photo, taken by Sgt Jimmy Mapham at around 08:45 on the 6th, shows a view of Queen Red from Queen White. Carefully analysed in D-Day Then and Now, it shows men from a Beach Group (No. 84 Fd Coy, RE) in the foreground, distinguishable by the white bands around their helmets, and behind them 8th Fd Amb, RAMC, attached to 8th Inf Bde, and possibly men of 41 RM Cdo who were tasked with taking Lion-sur-Mer and linking up with Gold Beach.*

Below: *Jimmy Mapham's LCT lands on Queen Red at 08:00 along with 27th Armd Bde. A tank brews up on the beach—it could be a DD Sherman of 13th/18th Hussars, an AVRE from 79th Armd Div, or one of A Sqn 22nd Dragoons' flails. The two well-known villas place this as opposite WN 20—"Cod"— whose 50mm gun casemate is identified at **E**.*

Right: *A section of Queen White Beach at la Brèche. Vehicles have, in the main, cleared the beach and are moving along the road behind it (the D514). This road was essential for movement because of the flooding of the land behind the beaches.*

Below right: *Troops of 101st Beach Group dig in. To the right the large casemate of WN 18.*

Below and Opposite, bottom: *A disabled Sherman flail tank of 22nd Dragoons on the beach near the western end of Queen White on June 7. Note the steel matting laid on the sand to provide a firm path towards the beach exit. The attrition of armor on the beach was significant until the strongpoints and their anti-tank weapons were cleared. Armor on Sword Beach was provided by A Sqn, 22nd Dragoons (the Sherman Crabs), 77th and 79th Sqns, 5th Assault Regt, RE (the AVREs), the DD Shermans belonged to the 13th/18th Hussars, and the Centaurs of 5th Ind RM Armd Support Bty. 33 of the 40 DD Shermans reached the beach safely, but the anticipated armored thrust toward Caen did not materialize mainly because of the logjams on the beaches (see photo **opposite, bottom**). These were caused by a combination of factors: the lack of space caused by higher tides than expected; the difficulties the beach parties had to provide secure lanes for exit through the obstacles and mines; the flooded terrain behind; and the strength of the defenses, not just on the beaches but inland.*

Right: *The Commandos of 1st SpS Bde reached the beach at around 08:20 on Queen Red (note the distinctive three-story Maison de la Mer (at A) that appears in many Sword photos).*

Below right: *Wire defences at the top of the beach between strongpoints WN 18 and WN 20 were easily breached but were often backed up by minefields. In the background Commandos from 1st SpS Bde are coming ashore to join the mass of men and vehicles squeezed onto the beach.*

Bottom right: *Traffic jams are beginning to build up along the lateral road behind the beach. This view is looking westward towards the junction with the main road to Hermanville. The tall building just visible in the top center of the picture is the present day Hotel on the Place du Cuirasse Courbet (see page 175).*

Inset: *3rd Inf Div identification badge.*

Order of Battle

British 3rd Inf Div

8th Bde
1st Bn, South Lancashire Regt
2nd Bn, East Yorkshire Regt
1st Bn, Suffolk Regt

9th Bde
2nd Bn, Lincolnshire Regt
1st Bn, King's Own Scottish Borders
2nd Bn, Royal Ulster Rifles

185th Bde
2nd Bn, Royal Warwickshire Regt
1st Bn, Royal Norfolk Regt
2nd Bn, King's Shropshire Light Infantry

Divisional Troops
3rd Recce Regt, RAC
3rd Div Engr
3rd Div Sigs
7th, 33rd, and 76th Fd, 20th A/Tk, and 92nd LAA Regts, RA
2nd Bn, Midlesex Regt (MG)

Attached
22nd Dragoons, 79th Armd Div
27th Ind Armd Bde (13/18th Royal Hussars, 1st East Riding Yeomanry, The Staffordshire Yeomanry)

1st Special Service Bde
Nos 3, 4, and 6 Cdo and No 45 RM Cdo

4th Special Service Bde
Nos 41, 46, 47, and 48 RM Cdo
10th Inter-Allied Cdo
5th RM Armd Support Regt

Below: Aerial view, taken on June 3, of the western part of "Cod," showing the maze of zig-zag trenches that linked the main positions of the fortification. Both the S Lancs and E Yorks regiments' landings were affected by this strongpoint near the junction of Queen Red and White beaches. Indeed, S Lancs lost its CO, a company commander, and his 2IC during the landing, and sustained over 100 other casualties. Assaulted by men of both regiments, with armor support, "Cod" fell at around 10:00.

Above: Anti-tank gun emplacement at the top of Queen beach. It is probably the 50mm weapon located on the eastern edge of "Cod."

Left: *Infantry from a beach group at the top of Queen White Beach on June 7. This photo was taken some 200 yards east of the Place du Cuirasse Courbet (below).*

Below, left and right, and Bottom:
A *Monument dedicated to the Allied Navy sailors who died during the landings.*

B and Below left: *Centaur memorial. Originally a dozer it was restored at Duxford, using the turret from a Cavalier. The turret numbers were to help battery commanders firing from landing craft in the run up to the beaches.*

C *Place du Cuirasse Courbet with 3rd Inf Div and S Lancs Regt memorials.*

D and Below *AVRE parked next to a distinctive building in the Place.*

1st Suffolks was the reserve battalion on Sword Beach and tasked with taking three strongpoints on the outskirts of Colleville (now Colleville-Montgomery): WN 16, codenamed "Morris," a battery of four 100mm guns in three H669 bunkers. This (according to the Suffolks' War Diary) "had already received heavy bombing by the RAF and after only a few rounds had been fired the garrison of about 60 Germans came out and surrendered. 'B' Coy then moved in and occupied the posn." Next, " 'A' Company, with one pl of 'D' Coy under comd for breaching, then moved up through the village to attack and capture the second locality just to the south" ("Daimler"). This left the strongest of the defensive positions: WN 18 "Hillman," the HQ of the German 736th Grenadier Regt, with two buried Type 608 concrete command bunkers, a Type 605 gun bunker, a number of MG Tobruks, all linked by trenches, surrounded by minefields and barbed wire. After an initial attack failed, a second assault was supported by 13th/18th Hussars' Shermans and this carried the position. The Germans surrendered, but the Hussars lost two tanks and the Suffolks lost two officers killed, along with five men, and 24 men wounded. The hero of the action was Pte J.R. "Bunker" Hunter who won a DCM for bravery in the action, while knocking out single-handedly the metal cupola of the regimental command bunker.

Top and Above: *Two views of "Morris" after capture.*

Right: *One of the Type 608 command bunkers at "Hillman," today a museum maintained by Les Amis du Suffolk Regiment. Note the opening of a Tobruk.*

Inset: *Plan of "Hillman" showing: 1 Memorial above Type 605 gun bunker; 2 Well; 3 Cistern; 4 Road bridge over trench; 5 Eastern guard post; 6 Kitchens; 7 Command Post A (Type 608) with cupola; 8 Northern Guard post beside road; 9/14/18 Type H58c Tobruks; 10 Command Post B (Type 608); 19 Encircling barbed wire and minefield; 20 Trench system; 11–17 other underground bunkers not part of museum.*

N

Minefield

14

9

10

11

7

8

3

15

13

4

6

12

2

5

16

18

17

1

Minefield

0   100 YARDS

Top left: *Piper Millin (A) pipes the 1st SpS Bde ashore. Lord Lovat is at B. Millin would be at Lovat's side when the commandos linkup up with the paras at Bénouville.*

Top right: *Lt-Col The Lord Lovat, commander of No 4 Commando, his trusty hunting rifle slung across his shoulder and wearing a comfortable pair of corduroy trousers, talks to Brig Laycock at Newhaven after his return from the Dieppe raid.*

Above: *Commandos following a 13th/18th Hussar DD Sherman on the way to Ouistreham.*

Right: *Commandos resting near the Hillman strongpoint.*

Above: *Commandant Kieffer and his men make their way toward Ouistreham.*

Far left: *Troops digging in on the southern edge of 6th Airborne's drop zone at Ranville, on June 6. Horsa gliders can be seen in the background. The men in the foreground are believed to be from HQ Coy of 1st Royal Ulster Rifles, 6th Airlanding Bde. Linking up with 1st SpS Bde commandos helped to keep the east flank of the invasion bridgehead secure.*

Left: *No 4 Cdo and Combined Operations cloth badges.*

Below left: *Commandos and Paras link up. They would fight desperately to take the high ground on the eastern flank of the invasion bridgehead and hold it in the face of German counterattacks. The main action centered on Bréville. After the village was captured in a short, bitter action on June 12/13 by a mixed force supported by tanks of the 13th/18th Royal Hussars and five regiments of artillery, the German counterattacks ceased.*

180

Opposite: *Philippe Kieffer's commandos—the 177 men of the 1st BFM Commando—were integrated into the No 4 Cdo. Landing on Queen Red Beach, 21 were killed and 93 wounded in the attacks on strongpoints in Ouistreham. Erected in 1984 on top of a WN 10 turret, this steel flame commemorates the 1st SpS Bde soldiers who lost their lives. Etched into the flame are the names of the French Commandos of No 4 Cdo and on the slope below are markers for the nine French commandos of Kieffer's Brigade who died on this beach.*

Above: A *The Merville Battery (see pages 74–75).*
B *Franceville Strongpoint 05 defended the eastern flank of the entrance to the port of Ouistreham. The site included a 1779 French fort, which had a tank turret mounted on top and* another in the middle of the fort. There are fire control posts, crew quarters and various other bunkers, including ...
C *A Type H612 casemate, which enfiladed the estuary.*
D *WN 07 defended the entrance to Ouistreham port.*
E *Today a museum, the 52-feet-high "Grand Bunker Musée Le Mur d'Atlantique," was designed as a flak tower to control the AA defense of the harbor and was in control of the batteries covering the port. After suffering heavy casualties trying to take the tower, it finally fell on June 9 to Lt Bob Orrell of 91st Fd Coy, RE.*
F *The Kieffer Flame.*

Above: *On the western edge of Sword Beach, No 41 Cdo (seen here) was tasked with taking the WN 21 strongpoint "Trout" and then the chateau at Lion-sur-Mer before linking up with troops from Juno Beach. The secondary objective was to take the radar station at Douvres. The first stage—"Trout"—proved to be straightforward because the enemy had fled. The chateau proved more difficult and the linkup did not happen until the 7th. Reinforced by the Lincolnshires and the Royal Ulster Rifles, 41 Cdo liberated Lion-sur-Mer and marched on Luc-sur-Mer. However, units of 21st Pz Div had also reached the area, although in small numbers —one Kampfgruppe (Oppeln) had lost a number of tanks to the Staffordshire Yeomanry, to 41st A/Tk Bty, RA at Biéville, and men of the 185th Bde on the Periers Ridge, and had been forced to take up a defensive position. Kampfgruppe Rauch, however, reached the sea, but when reinforcements failed to arrive, and when 249 gliders crossed the shoreline (**Opposite, above left**) the Panzers were concerned they would be surrounded so withdrew.*

182

Above right and Right: *The sundial memorial to 41 RM Commando at Lion-sur-Mer. Nearby is a Churchill AVRE.*

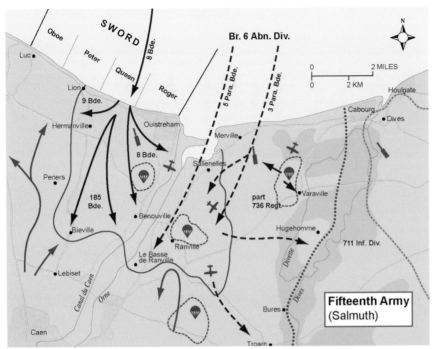

Map labels (above left):

SWORD

Oboe · Peter · Queen · Roger

8 Bde.

Br. 6 Abn. Div.

5 Para. Bde.

3 Para. Bde.

N

0 ——— 2 MILES
0 ——— 2 KM

Luc · Lion · 9 Bde. · Hermanville · Ouistreham · Houlgate

8 Bde. · Merville · Cabourg · Dives

Periers · 185 Bde. · Sallenelles

Bieville · Benouville · Varaville · Hugehomme

Le Basse de Ranville · Ranville · part 736 Regt.

Caen · Lebiset · 711 Inf. Div.

Canal du Caen · Orne · Divette · Dives · Bures · Troarn

Fifteenth Army (Salmuth)

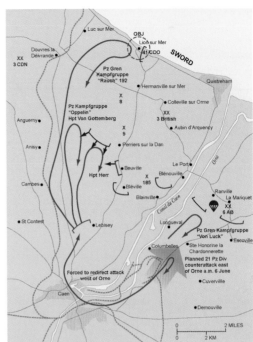

Map labels (above right):

Luc sur Mer · OBJ · Lion sur Mer · 41 CDO · SWORD

Douvres la Délivrande · XX 3 CDN

Pz Gren Kampfgruppe "Rauch" 192 · Hermanville sur Mer · Quistreham

Pz Kampfgruppe "Oppeln" Hpt Von Gottemberg · Colleville sur Orme · XX 3 British

Anguerny · X 8 · X 9 · Aubin d'Arquency

Anisy · Perriers sur la Dan · Le Port · Blénouville

Hpt Herr · Beuville · Ranville · La Mariquet · XX 6 AB

Campes · X 185 · Bléville · Blainville

St Contest · Longueval · Pz Gren Kampfgruppe "Von Luck"

Lebisey · Columbelles · Ste Honorine la Chardonnerette · Escoville

Forced to redirect attack west of Orne · Planned 21 Pz Div counterattack east of Orne a.m. 6 June

Caen · Cuverville · Demouville

Canal du Caen · Orne

0 ——— 2 MILES
0 ——— 2 KM

Above left: *Map showing operations on Sword Beach and Orne River.*

Above right: *Map showing 21st Panzer Div's advance to the sea.*

Left: *A 21st Pz Div Marder hurries past a British glider. The division had been split into three, with Von Luck's Kampfgruppe attacking the Airborne troops on the eastern banks of the Orne and Kampfgruppen Oppeln and Rauch attacking towards Lion-sur-Mer as mentioned opposite..*

Inset: *21st Pz Div's tactical sign.*

Below: *Kampfgruppe Rauch and Oppeln attacked between Sword and Juno. It was the latter that suffered badly at the hands of the Staffordshire Yeomanry and was ordered into a defensive line, where this PzKpfw IV Ausf H was knocked out on July 13.*

CHAPTER 10
IN MEMORIAM

"We, once conquered by William, have now set free the Conqueror's native land."

Latin epitaph on the frieze of the Bayeux Memorial

Below: *The Bayeux Commonwealth War Graves Commission Cemetery.*

Above: *The Colleville cemetery closes at 17:00 each day with the playing of the Last Post by a bugler.*

Above right and Opposite: *The American dead were laid to rest in the beautiful American Cemetery in the village of Colleville-sur-Mer overlooking Omaha Beach. There's a memorial, a semicircular colonnade with a loggia at each end containing large maps and narratives of the military operations (identified A); at the center is the bronze statue, "Spirit of American Youth." Since May 2007 there's been a visitor center to tell the story of the 9,387 Americans buried here (B). On the bluff to the east are the Big Red One memorial (opposite, C) and the 5th Engineer Special Brigade memorial atop WN 62 (D).*

Above right and Right: *While it is invidious to pick out any single grave, it is worth drawing attention to that of Brig-Gen Theodore Roosevelt, Jr. (see page 82). Among those buried in the cemetery are more than 300 unknown soldiers.*

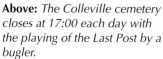

186

Above: *There are two major Canadian war grave cemeteries in Normandy. The one at Bény-sur-Mer (above) has a total of 2,048 burials. A larger cemetery at Cintheaux has 2,793 Canadian soldiers buried within, 91 of them unknown. With them lie 79 members of the RCAF.*

Above and Right: *The largest World War II Commonwealth cemetery at Bayeux, with 4,648 burials, is opposite the Bayeux Memorial (seen here). More than 1,800 Commonwealth dead with no grave are honored here. There's a Latin epitaph on the frieze:*

"We, once conquered by William, have now set free the Conqueror's native land." In addition to the Commonwealth burials, there are 466 graves of German soldiers at Bayeux.

THE NAMES OF THE
SOLDIERS OF THE
BRITISH COMMONWEALTH
AND EMPIRE
WHO FELL IN THE
ASSAULT UPON THE
NORMANDY BEACHES
OR IN THE
SWEEP TO THE SEINE
BUT TO WHOM
THE FORTUNE OF WAR
DENIED A KNOWN
AND HONOURED GRAVE
ARE RECORDED UPON
THESE WALLS
6TH JUNE — 29TH AUGUST 1944

Left and Below: *The cemetery at La Cambe was first set up by the US Army Graves Registration Service. After the war, the American dead were either transferred to Colleville or repatriated. After the 1954 Franco-German Treaty on War Graves, the remains of 12,000 German soldiers were moved in to La Cambe from 1,400 locations in Brittany and Normandy. There are upward of 21,000 buried here, including SS-Hauptsturmführer Michael Wittmann. The central tumulus is surmounted by a dark basalt cross flanked by two statues.*

BIBLIOGRAPHY

Books, Magazines, and Online Publications

Abraham, Capt. Robert: *The Operations of the 508th Parachute Infantry (82nd Airborne Division) Normandy, France, 5–10 June 1944*; Infantry School, Fort Benning, GA, 1948.

American Forces in Action: *Omaha Beachhead (6 June–13 June 1944)*; Center of Military History, US Army, Washington, D.C., 1994.

American Forces in Action: *Utah Beach to Cherbourg 6–27 June 1944*; Center of Military History, US Army, Washington, D.C., 1990.

Bennett, Ralph: *Behind the Battle: Intelligence in the War with Germany 1939–1945*; Pimlico, London, 1999.

Bernage, Georges: *Red Devils in Normandy*; Editions Heimdal, Bayeux, France, 2002.

Bird Battlefield Tours: D-Day Tour, 2007.

Bowman, Martin W: *Remembering D-Day: Personal Histories of Everyday Heroes*; HarperCollins, London, 2004.

Buffetaut, Yves: *Les Panzers en Normandie*; Histoire & Collections, Paris, France, 1991.

Burgett Donald R.: *Currahee!: A Screaming Eagle at Normandy*; Dell Publishing Company, 2000.

Bureau of Medicine and Surgery: *The US Navy Medical Department at War 1941–1945*; via http://www.ibiblio.org/hyperwar/USN/Admin-Hist/068B-Med/

Charbonnier, Philippe (compiler): *6 June 1944 Soldiers in Normandy*; Histoire & Collections, Paris, France, 1994.

Chazette, Alain: *Le Mur de l'Atlantique en Normandie*; Editions Heimdal, Bayeux, France, 2000.

Crookenden, Napier: *Dropzone Normandy*; Ian Allan Ltd, Shepperton, UK, 1976.

Ellis, Chris: *Spearhead 1: 21st Panzer Division*; Ian Allan Ltd, Hersham, UK, 2001.

Ellis, John: *World War II: The Sharp End*; Windrow & Greene, London, 1990.

_____: *Brute Force: Allied Strategy and Tactics in the Second World War*; André Deutsch, London, 1990.

Ford, Ken: *Campaign 105: D-Day 1944 (3) Sword Beach & the British Airborne Landings*; Osprey Publishing Ltd, Oxford, UK, 2002.

_____: *Campaign 112: D-Day 1944 (4) Gold & Juno Beaches*; Osprey Publishing Ltd, Oxford, UK, 2002.

Gawne, Jonathan: *Spearheading D-Day American Special Units of the Normandy Invasion*; Histoire & Collections, Paris, France, 1998.

Hastings, Max: *Overlord*; Papermac, London, 1993.

Hendley, LT(jg) Coit, USCGR: *Report of the action of the USS LCI (L) 85 during Operation Neptune*; via http://www.uscg.mil/history/Normandy_Index.asp

Hills, Stuart: *By Tank into Normandy*; Cassells & Co, London, 2002.

Hogg, Ian V.: *British & American Artillery of World War Two*; Greenhill Books, London, 2002.

Holt, Tonie and Valmai: *Major & Mrs Holt's Battlefield Guide: Normandy Landing Beaches*; Leo Cooper, Barnsley, 1999.

Jarymowycz, Roman J.: "Der Gegenangriff Vor Verrieres: German Counterattacks during Operation Spring, 25–26 July 1944," *Canadian Military History*: Vol. 2: Iss. 1, Article 6, 1993 via http://scholars.wlu.ca/cmh/vol2/iss1/6

Kershaw, Robert J.: *D-Day: Piercing the Atlantic Wall*; Ian Allan Ltd, Hersham, UK, 1993.

Keusgen, Helmut k. von: *Pointe du Hoc*; Editions Heimdal, Bayeux, France, 2006.

McNorgan, Michael R.: *The Gallant Hussars: A History of the 1st Hussars Regiment 1856–2004*; 1st Hussars Cavalry Fund, 2004.

Montgomery, FM the Viscount: *Normandy to the Baltic*; Hutchinson & Co Ltd, 1946.

Overy, Richard: *Why the Allies Won*; Pimlico, London, 1995.

Ramsey, J.: *D-Day Memories of a Tank Gunner: With 'A' Squadron Westminster Dragoons*; via http://www.bbc.co.uk/history/ww2peopleswar/stories/89/a2698789.shtml

Ramsey, Winston G.: *D-Day Then and Now*; two volumes, *After the Battle*, London, 1995.

Richardson, Jack: *The Normandy Landings, 6 June 1944: Royal Marines*; via http://www.bbc.co.uk/history/ww2peopleswar/stories/58/a2174258.shtml

Shulman, Milton: *Defeat in the West*; Pan Books Ltd, London, 1988.

Small, Ken: *The Forgotten Dead*; Bloomsbury, London, 1989.

Stacey, O.B.E, Colonel C.P.: *The Canadian Army at War, Canada's Battle in Normandy, The Canadian Army's Share in the Operations, 6 June–1 September 1944*; Department of National Defense, 1946 via http://www.ibiblio.org/hyperwar/UN/Canada/CA/Normandy/

The History of IX Engineer Command From its beginning to V-E Day, 1945 via http://www.ixengineercommand.com/

United States Coast Guard: *The Coast Guard At War. V. Transports and Escorts. Vol. 2;* Washington: Public Information Division, Historical Section, U.S. Coast Guard Headquarters, 1949 via http://www.uscg.mil/history/Normandy_Index.asp

Vanderveen, Bart: *Historic Military Vehicles Directory*; After the Battle, London, 1989.

Various: *Untold Stories of D-Day*; *National Geographic Magazine*, June 2002.

Warren, Dr. John C.: *USAF Historical Studies 97 Airborne Operations in World War II, European Theater*; USAF Historical Division, 1956.

Westwell, Ian: *Spearhead 6: 1st Infantry Division*; Ian Allan Ltd, Hersham, UK, 2002.

_____: *Spearhead 12: US Rangers*; Ian Allan Ltd, Hersham, UK, 2003.

Winser, John de S.: *The D-Day Ships*; World Ship Society, Kendal, UK, 1994.

Zaloga, Steven J.: *Campaign 100: D-Day 1944 (1) Omaha Beach*; Osprey Publishing Ltd, Oxford, UK, 2003.

Zaloga, Steven J.: *Campaign 104: D-Day 1944 (2) Utah Beach & the US Airborne Landings*; Osprey Publishing Ltd, Oxford, UK, 2004.

Zaloga, Steven J.: *Fortress 37: D-Day Fortifications in Normandy*; Osprey Publishing Ltd, Oxford, UK, 2005.

Web resources

http://www.flickr.com/photos/photosnormandie/sets/72157632757723303/: collection of well-captioned photos mostly from official sources

http://academic.mu.edu/meissnerd/atlanticwall.html

http://forum.axishistory.com/

http://warchronicle.com/

http://ww2images.blogspot.co.uk/2013_04_01_archive.html

http://www.dday-overlord.com/

http://www.feldgrau.net

http://www.oisterwijk-marketgarden.com/ww2_trips_and_museum_visits.html

http://www.strijdbewijs.nl/

http://www.war44.com/omaha-beach/310-bloody-omaha.html

http://www.warchronicle.com/dday/utah/ivy.htm#4th

http://www.warhistoryonline.com/

http://1-22infantry.org/: Unit info

http://508pir.org/index.htm: Info on 508th PIR.

http://casfcaps.freehosting.net/capbadges3.htm: Canadian badges

http://fighter-collection.com/cft/: Info on aircraft.

http://royal-ulster-rifles-ww2.blogspot.co.uk/p/gallery.html: Official history of 2 RUR during World War 2

http://www.29infantrydivision.org/: Info on 29th Inf Div

http://www.506infantry.org/: Info on the Currahees—506th PIR

http://www.atlantikwall.org.uk/: Comprehensive site on fortifications and batteries.

http://www.galik.com/stanleygalik1922/about/: Story of Stanley Galik and LCI (L) 35

http://www.historynet.com/world-war-ii-interview-with-101st-air-borne-trooper-james-flanagan-about-d-day.htm: James Flanagan info.

http://www.lstmemorial.org/wayitwas.htm: History of LST-325.

http://www.mapleleafup.ca/dday5-2ndwave.html: Info on CFPU photos and photographers

http://www.navsource.org/archives/10/16/160325.htm: Info on individual ships.

http://www.petergh.f2s.com/flashes.html: Excellent listing of British badges.

http://www.ronaldv.nl/abandoned/airfields/FR/lowernormandy/calvados.html: Info on airfields.

http://zulukilo.wordpress.com/2010/06/06/the-bridge-at-la-fiere/: Story of what happened at La Fière.

CREDITS

The authors would like to thank all those who helped with the material for the book, particularly Mark Franklin who did the maps; Jan Suermondt for the artwork. Other sources are listed below (apologies if we've missed or incorrectly identified anyone): AFP/Getty Images 73767948 124B; Peter Anderson 67BR, 71 inset B, 89R, 119 CR & BR, 144B, 180BL & BR, 186TL; Eric Bates 140C; Battlefield Historian 126C, 131B, 133TR, 134B, 135 all, 141 all, 145C, 146–147, 152C, 156B, 164C, 170B, 172T, 173B, 174 both, 175T, 176 both, 178CR, 179T, 182T, 183T; Bundesarchiv 21C, 165T, C, & B; via S Dunstan 179CR, 179B; FDR Presidential Library & Museum 9T; George Forty Collection 4 inset, 8, 15, 18BL, 19B, CL & CR, 29B, 46T, 54BL, 68B, 72BR, 74T, 77B, 100, 104T, 116TL, 119BL, 121B, 130T, 130C, 134C, 136T, 152BL & BR, 158B, 183B, 189T; Greene Media 49R, 77T; 9B, 16, 21T, 30CL, 30 CR, 31B, 34 inset, 36TL, 37B, 40 both, 68T, 69 inset, 69TL, 69TR, 71T, 72T, 72BL, 75TR, 76 inset, 76B, 133L, 136–137B, 137T, 138TL, 140B, 143T & B, 157B, 163B, 166–167, 171 both, 172C 172B, 173T, 173C, 175CR, 178T, C, & B, 178 C, 178B, 179CL, 183BR; Library of Congress 11, 17T; MilborneOne via Wiki-Commons 36B; NARA 4, 10, 13 BR, 17B, 20 all, 22–23, 24B, 25B, 26–27; 26B, 27 inset T, 28, 30T, 31T, 34C, 35, 36CL, 36TR, 37T &TR, 38–39, 41 all, 42 CLB, 43T, 46B, 47, 48, 50T, 50C, 51 all, 52, 55 all, 56T, 56B, 59B, 60–61, 62–63, 64B, 65, 66T, 67T, 67BL, 80–81, 82T, 82L, 84TL, 84AL, 84BR, 85, 86T, 86–87, 87 insets, 88C & B, 89T, CL, & BL, 90T, 92T, 93 all, 94 both, 95B, 96B, 97 both, 98–99, 103B, 105TR, 106–107 all, 108–109, 108 TR, 110B, 111B, 112–113, 112C, 113 TR & CR, 114–115, 116CL, 116C & B, 117 all, 118 all, 120 all, 121T, 122–123, 125B, 128–129, 130B, 131T, 132 both, 133B, 134T, 137B, 138TR, 139T, 145T, 148, 150BL, 151BL & BR, 152T, 160T, 168–169; National Archives of Canada 25TR & CR, 31C, 34B (RCAF), 78, 79T, 79BL & BR, 149, 153B, 154T, 154C, 154BL, 154BR, 155 all, 156T & inset, 157T, 157C, 158T, 159C & B, 160C, 162B, 163T & C, 164T, 164B, 165BR; Jean-Marc Poirier via Wiki Commons 1; USAMHI 49L; USCG 42T & CR; SSgt. Perry Heimer, US Army 186C; US Navy 42CLT, 42B, 42BL, 43B, 138–139B; US Signal Corps 50B, 88T; SSgt Marie Cassetty, USAF 186B; TSgt Timothy Cook, USAF 57B, 92B; A1C Steven Czyz, USAF 54 TL, 54CL; www.nmbs2001.com 130C; Wikipedia 83T, 83B, 102T & 103T; Burtonpe at en.wikipedia 188T; Nick-D via Wikipedia 184–185; DennisPeeters via Wikipedia 188R; Pinpin via Wikipedia 188L; Richard Wood 54CL; http://www.flickr.com/photos/gouldy/; Xfig-power via Wikipedia 96T.

Below left: *Flying's a great way to see and photograph the battlefields—but you need a pilot. Leo has the right credentials.*

Below right: *Cycling is a pretty good—if slower—alternative, trouble is it's easy to fall among thieves.*

INDEX